MINDGASM

A Lighthearted Yet Comprehensive Self-Help Guide to Sexual Transmutation, Energy, and Unlocking Your Potential

Tony Marino

Contents

INTRODUCTION: AN ORDINARY GUY WITH EXTRAORDINARY LESSONS 4

PREFACE 6

INTRODUCTION: EMBRACING THE HIDDEN POWER 8

CHAPTER 1 13

Understanding Sexual Energy: Beyond the Bedroom, Beyond the Myths 13

CHAPTER 2 19

Historical Perspectives: East Meets West - From Taoist Secrets to Modern Psychology 19

CHAPTER 3 29

Influential Thinkers and Cultural Practices: From Renaissance Masters to Netflix-Era Gurus 29

CHAPTER 4 38

The Science Behind Sexual Energy: Hormones, Brain Waves, and the Alchemy of Arousal 38

CHAPTER 5 47

Expanding Creativity and Productivity: Turning Desire into Your Muse 47

CHAPTER 6 54

Emotional Resilience, Confidence, and Well-Being: Building Your Inner Fortress with Sexual Transmutation 54

CHAPTER 7 62

Relationship Harmony and Intimacy: Transmuting Desire for Deeper Connections 62

CHAPTER 8 70

Spiritual Growth and Higher Consciousness: Ascending Beyond the Physical 70

CHAPTER 9 78

Preparing Your Mind: Mindset, Mindfulness, and Motivation
.... 78

CHAPTER 10 85

Core Techniques for Harnessing Sexual Energy: Your
Roadmap to Daily Practice.. 85

CHAPTER 11 92

Guided Meditations, Breathwork, and Solo Practices:
Deepening Your Personal Exploration............................ 92

CHAPTER 12 102

Partnered Exercises and Deeper Intimacy: Harnessing
Desire as a Dynamic Duo... 102

CHAPTER 13 111

Applying Sexual Transmutation in Daily Life: From Mundane
to Mind-Blowing 111

CHAPTER 14 118

Advanced Practices, Rituals, and Spiritual Traditions:
Taking Transmutation to the Next Level 118

CHAPTER 15 126

Overcoming Challenges, Taboos, and Pitfalls: Navigating
the Bumps on Your MINDGASM Journey...................... 126

CHAPTER 16 133

Ethics, Boundaries, and Professional Contexts: Keeping
MINDGASM Responsible and Respectful 133

THE MINDGASM TOOLKIT 141

INTRODUCTION: AN ORDINARY GUY WITH EXTRAORDINARY LESSONS

Hey there, I'm Tony Marino, and before we dive in, let me just say I'm an ordinary guy. No fancy titles, no long list of credentials to impress you. What I do have is a lot of curiosity and a passion for growth that has led me on a journey I could never have predicted.

Mindgasm isn't just a book it's the result of years of my own research, study, and countless conversations with people from all walks of life. I've spoken with artists, influencers, business leaders, parents, teachers, spiritual thinkers, and just regular folks trying to get through life with a little more joy and success. I've read lots of books, sifted through some of history's greatest lessons, and spent time surveying what truly works when it comes to personal development and transformation.

What I've discovered is simple: nobody has a monopoly on good ideas. We're all on this journey of life together, and it's through sharing, caring, and learning from one another that we grow. This book is my way of sharing some of the most powerful tools, insights, and lessons I've gathered along the way. I've applied them in my own life, and I'm still on the journey of personal development as I'm sure you are too. It's far from over, but these ideas have been game-changers for me, and I believe they might just hit the spot for you, too. Literally!

You'll see contributions from a wide range of people, stories from history, and a mashup of insights that might just hit you like a bolt of lightning or in this case, a *mindgasm*. Now, I'm not a therapist or a doctor, and nothing in this book should be taken as professional or medical advice. This is a collection of ideas and experiences, the kind that anyone, yes, even you can share with the world. What you choose to take from it is entirely up to you. In the end, you're the one who decides how these lessons fit into your life or not. You're a grown up so you decide.

In this interconnected world, we're all figuring it out together. Life comes with its fair share of trials and tribulations, but if there's one thing I've learned, it's that we're all a lot more powerful than we give ourselves credit for. *Mindgasm* is my way of serving up some self-help with authenticity, honesty, and a little bit of cheekiness. Take what resonates with you and leave the rest.

So, are you ready to dive in? Let's go on this journey together, and who knows you might just discover this ordinary guy put you onto something extraordinary.

Tony Marino

PREFACE

Helloooooo and welcome to *MINDGASM*! If that title made you raise an eyebrow or let out a cheeky little chuckle, you're already in the right headspace. Think of this book as your friendly, slightly mischievous companion on a journey to discover the **transformative** power of your own sexual energy. Yes, you read that correctly: we're going to talk about sex but not in the way you might expect.

Some of you might be thinking, "Sexual energy? Isn't that just... wanting to get it on?" Well, sure. But that's only the tip of the iceberg. Underneath the surface of physical desire is a massive reservoir of **creative, life-giving, and mind-fueling** force that can be harnessed for just about any ambition. Ancient civilizations knew it. Modern psychologists are hinting at it. Successful entrepreneurs, artists, and spiritual seekers across time have tapped into it, whether consciously or unconsciously.

Yet, for all its potential, sexual energy is often misunderstood. We might relegate it to the realm of bedroom antics or, worse, bury it under layers of shame, guilt, and social taboo. This is where *MINDGASM* steps in, aiming to blow the dust off this topic, toss in a sprinkle of humor, and serve up a hearty dose of practical wisdom. Our goal? **To show you how to channel that raw, buzzing energy** into your relationships, career, personal development, and even your spiritual life.

What to Expect from This Book

1. **A Cheeky Yet Respectful Tone**: We'll joke and jest, because sex is often an absurdly taboo subject. But rest assured, we'll keep things respectful, mindful, and oriented toward personal growth.
2. **Historical and Scientific Insights**: You'll find references to ancient Taoist practices, Tantric traditions, and modern neuroscience. It's like a smorgasbord of wisdom from East to West.
3. **Practical Techniques and Exercises**: From breathing techniques to journaling prompts, you'll discover a variety of ways to explore and direct your sexual energy.

4. **Stories, Analogies, and the Occasional Anecdote**: Expect real-life examples (some fictionalized for privacy) illustrating how sexual transmutation can manifest in everyday life.

Who Is This Book For?

- **The Curious Self-Improver**: If you've read a stack of personal development books and are itching for something fresh, welcome aboard.
- **The Burnt-Out Achiever**: Tired of forcing productivity? Sexual transmutation might be the "secret sauce" that reignites your spark.
- **The Spiritually Inclined**: If you sense there's something divine or cosmic about sexual energy, we'll delve into that realm too.
- **Couples Seeking a Deeper Bond**: You and your partner might find new levels of intimacy and shared purpose through these teachings.

A Word on Style

Yes, the word "mindgasm" is a bit cheeky, but it's also deliberate. An orgasm is typically associated with a climax of pleasure an explosive release of tension. A *mindgasm*? That's when your **whole being** lights up, from the mental to the spiritual, as you direct your sexual energy to create or achieve something extraordinary. Think of it as that "Eureka!" moment, but fueled by a primal, delicious force that's always been inside you.

As you turn the pages, I invite you to **suspend any embarrassment** or preconceived notions. Let yourself be playful and open-minded. After all, this is about discovering new dimensions of yourself, dimensions that might just blow your mind (pun fully intended).

So, take a breath, maybe wiggle your shoulders to release any tension, and get ready to embark on a journey that's equal parts enlightening, fun, and (hopefully) life-changing. Let's do this!

INTRODUCTION: EMBRACING THE HIDDEN POWER

Picture this: You're sitting at your desk on a Tuesday afternoon, staring at a spreadsheet or a blank document. You feel that familiar lull like your brain is swimming through molasses. Suddenly, your phone buzzes with a flirty text from someone you're crushing on, or you recall a steamy scene from a movie. In a flash, your body tenses, your heart flutters, and your mind snaps to attention.

That's **sexual energy** making a cameo appearance in your everyday life. It's not just about the urge to do something physical. It's a rush a spark that can wake you up faster than a double espresso.

Sexual Energy: More Than Just Lust

Contrary to popular belief, sexual energy doesn't exist solely for hooking up or making babies. In many cultures ancient and modern it's viewed as **life force**. Think of it as rocket fuel: you can burn it quickly for a burst of speed, or you can harness it carefully for a more sustained and directed journey.

- **In Creative Work**: Artists have long talked about "muses" and "inspiration." Often, that spark of genius arises from the same wellspring as sexual desire an undercurrent of passion that begs to be expressed.

- **In Physical Achievements**: Athletes sometimes note that feeling of being "in the zone," a heightened state of presence and energy. Could sexual energy play a role there too? Quite possibly.

- **In Emotional Life**: Ever notice how feeling desired can boost your confidence? Or how a loving relationship can make you feel unstoppable? That's sexual energy in the emotional realm.

The Taboo That Keeps Us Stuck

So, if sexual energy is so helpful, why aren't we all out there channeling it into best-selling novels, innovative companies, or philanthropic endeavors? Because, quite frankly, **it's taboo**. We've been taught to hush it, confine it, or even fear it. And sure, boundaries are necessary nobody wants a world of inappropriate oversharing but we often swing too far in the other direction, squashing an entire dimension of human vitality.

When you start talking about using sexual energy to fuel your goals, some people might give you the side-eye, as if you're proposing a wild concept. But throughout this book, you'll see references to historical figures, spiritual teachers, and everyday folks who've tapped into this force intentionally or otherwise to do amazing things.

From Napoleon Hill to Netflix Binges

If you've ever read *Think and Grow Rich*, you might recall Napoleon Hill's famous chapter on "The Mystery of Sex Transmutation." He observed that some of the most successful people of his time seemed to possess a heightened level of **drive**, **charisma**, and **creative power** traits he linked to their ability to redirect sexual energy. Fast-forward to today: we have Netflix, dating apps, and a million distractions. The principle, however, remains the same. Sexual energy is like a generator. If you let it idle or waste it on fleeting dopamine hits, you lose its potential. But if you harness it like hooking it up to a power grid wow, can it light up your life.

The Mind-Body Connection

Science has jumped into the conversation too. Neuroscientists talk about **dopamine**, the "reward" neurotransmitter, which spikes during sexual arousal. Dopamine also motivates us to seek out rewards like finishing a project or learning a new skill. In essence, the same chemical that gets triggered by romantic or sexual cues can be **repurposed** to help you chase other forms of success.

- **Hormones** like testosterone and estrogen play roles in confidence, mood, and ambition in all genders.

- **Oxytocin**, sometimes called the "cuddle hormone," fosters bonding and trust. That sense of connection can be extended to your audience if you're a performer or your clients if you're an entrepreneur.

The Scope of This Book

We'll cover a wide spectrum: from the **ancient Taoist** practices of circulating energy through the body to the **modern psychologist** who sees sexual desire as a form of creative drive. We'll also talk about practical applications: how to use breathwork, visualization, and even everyday tasks to channel that spark.

Here's the roadmap:

1. **Foundations**: A deep dive into what sexual energy is, how various cultures have understood it, and what science says.

2. **Benefits**: Detailed chapters on creativity, emotional well-being, relationships, and spiritual growth each area can benefit from sexual transmutation.

3. **Techniques**: A rich toolkit of exercises breathwork, meditation, journaling, partnered practices so you can tailor the approach to your lifestyle and comfort level.

4. **Challenges & Ethics**: We'll address the potential pitfalls, ethical considerations (especially in professional contexts), and how to keep the practice safe and respectful.

5. **Mastery**: Long-term integration, advanced practices (like Kundalini awakening or Tantric rituals), and real-life stories of people who've transformed their lives through sexual transmutation.

Why "MINDGASM"?

Let's break it down:

- **Mind**: This journey involves a lot of introspection, mindset shifts, and conscious reprogramming of beliefs.
- **Gasm**: Typically associated with an explosive release of pleasure. But here, it's a playful reminder that harnessing sexual energy can lead to an **explosive expansion** of creativity, purpose, and achievement without necessarily needing a physical orgasm.

A Lighthearted Approach

While we'll reference scientific studies and spiritual teachings, this book aims to keep things **cheeky** (pun intended) and **down-to-earth**. Why? Because so much literature around sexual energy can feel either too clinical or too esoteric. Let's meet in the middle: a comfortable place where we can laugh about the weirdness of being human while also respecting the profound power that lies within us.

Your Role as the Explorer

Yes, you're about to explore uncharted territory in your psyche and body. It's normal to feel a mix of curiosity and apprehension. You might wonder:

- "What if I discover something I don't like about myself?"

- "What if this unleashes more desire than I can handle?"

- "What if my partner thinks I'm nuts for reading this?"

These questions are valid. But growth often happens just outside our comfort zones. Keep an open mind, experiment gently, and trust that you can always step back or slow down if it feels overwhelming.

Setting Intentions

Before diving into Chapter 1, take a moment to consider what you want out of this journey. Maybe you're looking to spice up your relationship, or perhaps you're aiming for a career breakthrough. Or maybe you're just curious about that intangible "something more" in life. Write it down or at least hold it in your heart. That intention will be your **guiding star** as we move forward.

A Quick Teaser of What's to Come

- **Chapter 1** will blow the lid off misconceptions about sexual energy and show you it's not just about lust or reproduction it's a multi-layered force that can shape your reality.

- **Chapter 2** travels through time, revealing how different cultures and historical figures have approached the harnessing of desire for greater purposes.

We'll keep building from there, adding layers of knowledge, practical steps, and personal stories until you have a **full toolkit** for transforming your life.

So, are you ready to harness that hidden power? Let's flip the page and begin our deep dive into the realm of sexual energy no shame, no guilt, just boundless potential waiting to be tapped.

CHAPTER 1

Understanding Sexual Energy: Beyond the Bedroom, Beyond the Myths

Let's cut right to the chase: sexual energy is often pigeonholed into "bedroom business." But, oh, dear reader, it's so much more than that. Picture it as a shimmering river that flows beneath your everyday thoughts and actions. Sometimes it's calm and gentle, other times it's raging rapids. Either way, it's there ready to be directed.

1.1 The Multifaceted Nature of Sexual Energy

1. Physical Urges

Yes, the immediate association with sexual energy is the tingle in your body when you see someone attractive or think a spicy thought. It's the tension that begs for release. But that's just one aspect like seeing only the tip of an iceberg.

2. Emotional Underpinnings

Ever notice how desire can make you feel confident, bold, or even playful? On the flip side, suppressed sexual energy can lead to irritability or a sense of "blah." Emotionally, sexual energy can be a driver of excitement, passion, and overall zest for life.

3. Mental Spark

Sexual energy can sharpen your mind. Think about how your thoughts sometimes race when you're turned on, or how you become laser-focused on the object of your desire. Channel that mental clarity into something else a project, a workout, a creative endeavor and you might be surprised at the results.

4. Spiritual Current

Many spiritual traditions talk about the **kundalini** or **life force** that sits coiled at the base of your spine, waiting to be awakened. Sexual desire is intimately tied to that concept. When you harness it, you can experience heightened awareness, deeper empathy, and even mystical states.

1.2 Busting Common Myths

1. **Myth**: "Sexual energy is only about intercourse or orgasm."

Reality: You can experience a rush of sexual energy while cooking, dancing, or brainstorming. It's not limited to sexual acts.

2. **Myth**: "Harnessing sexual energy means never having normal sex again."

Reality: This is not about denial or forced celibacy. It's about **choice** knowing you can direct that energy elsewhere when you want to.

3. **Myth**: "Transmutation is some weird cult practice."

Reality: Every major culture has recognized some form of energy redirection, from yogic breathwork to medieval alchemy. It's about personal growth, not dogma.

4. **Myth**: "You have to be an expert meditator or a monk."

Reality: If you can breathe, you can practice sexual transmutation. No monastery membership required.

1.3 The Energy Spectrum: From Raw Lust to Refined Passion

Picture a dial that goes from 0 to 10:

- **At 0**: You're disengaged, no desire, no spark maybe feeling apathetic or exhausted.

- **At 10**: You're so overwhelmed by lust you can't think straight. Your mind is basically screaming, "Now! Now! Now!"

The sweet spot for sexual transmutation is learning to hover around, say, a 4 to 7 on that scale. Enough desire to feel energized, but not so much that you're compelled to immediate release or impulsive action. That's where you can pause, breathe, and redirect.

1.4 Sexual Energy as a Creative Catalyst

1. The "Muse Effect"

Writers, painters, musicians often talk about muses enigmatic sources of inspiration. Sometimes these muses are people they find attractive, or even fantasies. Essentially, they're tapping into sexual energy to fuel creativity.

2. Think of Your Brain as a Canvas

Instead of letting desire swirl aimlessly, imagine painting with it. Let each stroke of the brush (or each word you type, each chord you play) be infused with that energy.

3. Practical Exercise: Sensual Brainstorming

Next time you have a creative block, close your eyes for a moment. Conjure up a sensual memory or daydream that makes you feel warm and tingly. Let that feeling build for 30 seconds then open your eyes and start brainstorming. No filter, just raw ideas. You might be amazed at the leaps your mind takes.

1.5 Recognizing Sexual Energy in Daily Life

1. Physical Cues:

A flutter in your stomach, a quickening of the heart, warmth spreading in your chest or lower abdomen. These can be signs your sexual energy is stirring.

2. Emotional Cues:

You might feel sudden confidence, excitement, or a hint of mischief. Or maybe you feel more playful, more open to adventure.

3. Situational Triggers:

It could be a flirty text, a romantic scene in a movie, or even an inspiring quote that resonates with passion. Identifying these triggers helps you see how often sexual energy arises in day-to-day life.

4. Channel vs. Suppress:

Many of us suppress it: "I shouldn't feel like this right now." Instead, try channeling it: "I'll use this spark to power through my next task."

1.6 A Lighthearted Analogy: The Sexual Energy "Garden Hose"

Let's say you have a garden hose that's pumping out water (sexual energy). You can:

Spray it randomly all over the yard (impulsive release, random daydreaming, or fleeting fantasies).

- **Kink the hose** to stop the flow entirely (suppression, guilt, shame).

- **Attach a sprinkler** that waters your entire garden methodically (transmutation distributing that energy to your creative projects, relationships, and goals).

Which method yields a healthier, more vibrant "garden" (i.e., your life)? The third option, of course. That's what sexual transmutation is all about.

1.7 The Potential Pitfalls of Ignoring This Force

1. Repression and Its Consequences

Bottling up sexual energy can lead to irritability, depression, or a sense of something missing. It's like capping a volcano. Eventually, it might erupt in unhealthy ways like addiction or misplaced anger.

2. Hyper-Focus on Physical Release

On the flip side, if you only see sexual energy as something that must be "spent" through intercourse or solo activity, you miss out on the chance to redirect it. It's like using your entire paycheck on one item instead of budgeting for broader life goals.

3. Social and Relational Issues

If your partner wants deeper intimacy but you only approach sexual energy as a quick fix for physical relief, emotional disconnection can grow. Transmutation invites a more **holistic** view.

4. Blocked Creativity and Stagnation

Feeling stuck in a rut? Check if you're ignoring or misusing your sexual energy. Sometimes a stagnant love life or suppressed desire can mirror stagnation in other life areas.

1.8 Real-Life Mini-Case: "Rebecca the Stressed-Out Student"

Rebecca is a grad student juggling research, part-time work, and a social life. She notices that whenever she's near a deadline, she also experiences heightened sexual thoughts almost like her body is searching for a stress release. Initially, she'd distract herself or "take care of it" physically, but she realized it was cutting into her work time.

Upon discovering sexual transmutation, Rebecca tried a new approach: when that energy surfaced, she'd do a quick breathwork exercise (inhaling slowly, imagining warm light moving from her lower abdomen to her brain). She'd then dive back into her research. She reported sharper focus, fewer stress spikes, and a surprising boost in her academic creativity. It was as if she turned a potential distraction into rocket fuel for her thesis.

1.9 Building Awareness: A 3-Day Challenge

For the next three days, keep a small notebook or a note-taking app on your phone. Whenever you feel a hint of sexual desire be it mild or intense jot down:

1. **Time & Situation**: "2 PM, reading a novel," or "9 AM, had a daydream while making coffee."

2. **Physical Sensations**: "Tingly in my chest," "Warmth in my belly," etc.

3. **Mood or Thoughts**: "Felt excited, had an urge to text someone flirty," or "Distracted, can't focus on work."

No judgment, no immediate attempts to redirect just observe and note. By the end of three days, you'll likely see patterns: maybe you feel a surge mid-morning or late at night. Maybe certain topics or triggers consistently stir your desire. This data becomes your **map**, helping you navigate the next phases of transmutation.

1.10 Conclusion: The Starting Point

Understanding sexual energy is the first step toward harnessing it. Realize it's not "good" or "bad" it simply **is**. Like any powerful resource, how you use it defines its impact on your life. Embrace the possibility that this energy, often overlooked or confined to the realm of physical intimacy, can be your **ally** in everything from creative breakthroughs to emotional resilience.

In the next chapter, we'll zoom out and see how different cultures and eras have perceived and practiced this phenomenon. By the time you finish Part I, you'll have a rich tapestry of perspectives that underscore one crucial point: sexual transmutation is a **universal** human capacity, not some fringe idea. And it's yours to explore starting right now.

CHAPTER 2

Historical Perspectives: East Meets West - From Taoist Secrets to Modern Psychology

If Chapter 1 was your gateway into the concept of sexual energy, Chapter 2 is your time machine. We're about to hop across continents and centuries to see how different cultures some you've probably never heard of approached the notion of harnessing sexual desire for something bigger than just, well, sex.

2.1 Ancient Taoist Teachings: "Chi," "Jing," and the Microcosmic Orbit

1. Foundations in Taoism

In ancient China, scholars and mystics saw the human body as a microcosm of the universe. "Chi" was the life force flowing through everything. "Jing" was your **vital essence**, closely tied to sexual and creative energy.

Taoist sages believed that by refining Jing (through certain breathing, movement, and mental practices), you could achieve **longevity**, **vitality**, and **spiritual clarity**.

2. The Microcosmic Orbit

A cornerstone practice in which you guide energy up the spine and down the front of the body in a continuous loop.

By including sexual arousal in this loop, practitioners believed they could "recycle" energy instead of "losing" it. Imagine it like a self-charging battery for your mind, body, and spirit.

3. **Anecdote**: The Emperor's Secret Manual

Legends speak of secret scrolls where emperors learned how to preserve their life force by minimizing ejaculatory release and maximizing internal circulation. While some accounts might be exaggerated, they reflect a broader cultural fascination with using sexual energy for health and power.

4. Modern-Day Relevance

Today, many people learn simplified Taoist practices (like Mantak Chia's "Healing Tao" system) to cultivate sexual energy for personal well-being and spiritual growth. Even if you're not aiming for immortality, you can still glean major benefits like increased stamina and a calmer mind.

2.2 Tantric Wisdom: Union Beyond the Physical

1. Tantra in a Nutshell

Originating in India, Tantra sees the entire universe as an interplay of **masculine** and **feminine** energies (often personified as Shiva and Shakti).

Sexual union in Tantra is a **sacred** act that merges these polarities, transcending the purely physical realm to touch spiritual unity.

2. Misconceptions

Western pop culture sometimes paints Tantra as endless "wild sex marathons." While Tantric practices can involve prolonged intimacy, the core goal is **mindful union** a sense of dissolving boundaries between self, partner, and the divine.

3. Key Tantric Techniques

• **Breath Synchronization**: Partners align their inhalations and exhalations, creating a shared rhythm that intensifies connection.

• **Slow Movement and Eye Gazing**: Instead of rushing, Tantrikas linger in each sensation, each glance, letting the energy build gradually.

• **Mantras and Yantras**: Chanting and focusing on sacred geometrical images can elevate sexual energy into spiritual insight.

4. Tantra for Singles

Yes, you can practice Tantra solo. By visualizing the masculine and feminine energies within you, you cultivate an **inner marriage** harmonizing your psyche, body, and soul.

2.3 Greek Eros, Roman Indulgence, and the Philosophical Angle

1. **Eros in Ancient Greece**

For the Greeks, Eros was more than just lust it was the driving force of creation, a primordial god who brought life and passion into the world.

Philosophers like Plato viewed erotic love as a stepping stone toward appreciating higher forms of beauty and truth (the "Ladder of Love").

2. **Roman Feasts and Fears**

Romans could be famously indulgent (think lavish feasts, bacchanals), yet they also had moralists who warned against letting lust overshadow reason.

The tension between indulgence and restraint laid the groundwork for discussions on how to **balance** desire with duty an early version of "transmutation," you might say.

3. **Stoic Influence**

Some Stoic philosophers advocated controlling passions to maintain inner peace. While not explicitly about sexual transmutation, their emphasis on **self-mastery** resonates with the concept of channeling desire rather than suppressing it.

2.4 Western Alchemy: Turning Base Desires into "Spiritual Gold"

1. **Metaphorical Alchemy**

Medieval and Renaissance alchemists are often depicted trying to turn lead into gold. Symbolically, "lead" can represent raw impulses, and "gold" can represent spiritual enlightenment or higher consciousness.

Alchemists used coded language to describe processes that, in part, referred to sexual energy. Terms like "the Red King" and "the White Queen" sometimes alluded to masculine and feminine forces uniting.

2. Influential Figures

• **Paracelsus** wrote about the power of vital spirits and the importance of balancing bodily energies.

• **Jacob Boehme** delved into mystical unions, bridging the gap between religious devotion and sexual symbolism.

3. The Hermetic Tradition

Hermetic texts often mention the concept "As above, so below," implying that cosmic energies reflect human energies. This gave rise to practices that combined astrology, alchemy, and sexual symbolism.

While some of these works remain cryptic, the underlying theme is the **transformation** of base human drives into refined spiritual and creative power.

2.5 Indigenous and Tribal Perspectives

1. Sacred Sexuality in Tribal Communities

Many indigenous cultures integrate fertility rites and communal ceremonies that celebrate sexuality as part of **life's sacred cycle**.

Such practices can involve dance, chanting, or symbolic representations of union, often intended to ensure the prosperity of crops, families, or entire tribes.

2. Shamanic Journeys

Some shamans use trance states occasionally induced by rhythmic drumming or natural hallucinogens to tap into primal energies. Sexual desire, in these contexts, might be woven into a **vision quest** or healing ritual.

While not all shamanic practices revolve around sexual energy, the principle of harnessing primal forces for communal benefit is akin to transmutation on a group scale.

3. Respect and Reciprocity

In many indigenous worldviews, personal power is tied to **responsibility**. If you harness sexual energy, you're also tasked with using it ethically never to harm, but to uplift. That ethos parallels the modern emphasis on consent and positive intention.

2.6 The Christian and Islamic Middle Ages: Asceticism vs. Hidden Streams

1. Medieval Christian Views

Official Church doctrine often emphasized celibacy for clergy, viewing sexual desire as a temptation.

Yet, within certain mystical Christian traditions (like some Gnostic sects), there were hints of channeling sexual desire toward divine love. These beliefs sometimes clashed with mainstream dogma.

2. Sufi Poetry in Islam

Mystics like Rumi and Hafiz used **erotic language** to describe union with the Divine. Lines that appear to praise a lover's beauty often serve as metaphors for God's grace.

While overt sexual acts might be regulated by religious law, the poetic tradition suggests an undercurrent of transmutation turning longing into spiritual ecstasy.

3. The Hidden Streams

Throughout the Middle Ages, small groups (some considered heretical) explored a union of body and spirit, referencing sexual energy as a conduit to higher truths.

This esoteric knowledge was often suppressed or forced underground, contributing to the aura of secrecy around sexual transmutation.

2.7 Modern Psychology Steps In

1. Freud and Libido

• Sigmund Freud famously spotlighted **libido** as a foundational drive in human behavior. While his theories were controversial, they opened the door to discussing how sexual energy influences creativity, neuroses, and personality development.

Freud's notion of "sublimation" parallels transmutation: redirecting sexual impulses into socially acceptable (and often highly productive) outlets.

2. Jung and the Collective Unconscious

Carl Jung expanded on Freud's ideas, suggesting libido is not just sexual but a **general psychic energy**.

Jung's emphasis on archetypes, dreams, and spirituality resonates with ancient traditions that saw desire as a cosmic force, not just a bodily urge.

3. Contemporary Therapy and Coaching

Modern therapists may encourage clients to harness sexual desire for self-esteem and creativity.

Life coaches sometimes incorporate sexual transmutation principles without necessarily labeling them as such when helping clients tap into motivation and personal power.

2.8 Case Spotlight: Napoleon Hill's "Sex Transmutation" Chapter

1. A Revolutionary Idea

Published in 1937, *Think and Grow Rich* soared in popularity. Hill's discussion of sexual transmutation was groundbreaking in a business-oriented book.

He observed that many highly successful individuals had "a highly developed sex nature," which they channeled into leadership, innovation, and ambition.

2. Why It Mattered

Hill's perspective validated the concept for Western readers who might have otherwise dismissed it as "exotic" or "unscientific."

It spurred a wave of interest in the idea that desire, if properly managed, could be a powerhouse for success rather than a moral or social liability.

3. Criticisms and Misinterpretations

Some critics argue that Hill's evidence was anecdotal, and that correlation doesn't prove causation.

Others misread the chapter as advocating for sexual repression. In truth, Hill advocated **redirection**, not denial.

2.9 The Modern Renaissance: Yoga Studios, Workshops, and Apps

1. Yoga Boom

As yoga spread globally, many practitioners discovered that certain poses and breathwork techniques awakened sexual energy.

Studios began offering specialized workshops on **Tantra Yoga** or "sacred sexuality," merging ancient wisdom with contemporary self-improvement.

2. Mindfulness Apps

In an era of smartphone apps, it's not uncommon to find guided meditations aimed at harnessing desire or "pelvic energy" for stress relief or creative boosts.

While some are gimmicky, others provide legitimate breathwork and visualization exercises reminiscent of Taoist or Tantric teachings.

3. Sexual Wellness and Tech

A surge in sexual wellness startups markets everything from "smart vibrators" to guided intimacy programs for couples, occasionally integrating transmutation concepts.

The mainstreaming of these ideas indicates a growing acceptance of sexual energy as a **wellness** resource, not a taboo.

2.10 Lessons from History: What We Can Learn

1. Universality

Across cultures and epochs, people recognized that sexual energy isn't purely about reproduction or fleeting pleasure. It's a **creative** and **spiritual** force.

2. Diversity of Approaches

There's no single "right" way to practice sexual transmutation. From Taoist alchemy to Tantric rituals, from Stoic self-mastery to Jungian sublimation, each tradition offers valuable insights.

3. Balancing Restraint and Expression

Too much indulgence can lead to chaos; too much suppression can lead to frustration. The sweet spot lies in **conscious redirection** a middle path of harnessing energy without letting it rule or ruin you.

4. Modern Adaptation

We have more resources than ever: online classes, cross-cultural knowledge, scientific backing. The question is whether we'll use them to unlock our potential or stay mired in taboos.

2.11 Practical Reflection: Find Your Philosophical Fit

Now that you've taken a whirlwind tour of how various cultures have tackled sexual transmutation, think about which perspective resonates most with you:

- **Taoist Circulation**: More body-focused, emphasizing breath and subtle energy flows.

- **Tantric Union**: A holistic blend of sensuality, spirituality, and relational depth.
- **Western Alchemy**: A symbolic approach, turning "base" impulses into "gold" of achievement or enlightenment.
- **Psychological Sublimation**: Grounded in modern therapy, focusing on channeling desire into creative or productive outlets.

There's no reason you can't sample from multiple traditions. Maybe you'll adopt Taoist breathwork but also find Jung's archetypes fascinating. Or you might love Tantric eye-gazing but resonate with Hill's pragmatic emphasis on success. This journey is yours customize it.

2.12 Bridging History to Your Present Practice

1. Embrace the Wisdom

Recognize that your pursuit of sexual transmutation places you in a long lineage of explorers from emperors to artists, from yogis to business magnates.

2. Avoid the "One True Way" Trap

Historical accounts can be inspiring but remember they were shaped by specific cultural and social contexts. Adapt and refine for your life situation.

3. Stay Open and Curious

The beauty of living in the modern era is that you have **unprecedented access** to knowledge. Keep learning, experimenting, and evolving.

2.13 Conclusion: A Tapestry of Timeless Wisdom

As you can see, the concept of channeling sexual energy isn't a random new-age trend. It's a tapestry woven from countless threads ancient, medieval, modern, Eastern, Western, mystical, and scientific. Whether you identify as more spiritual, more pragmatic, or somewhere in between, there's a place for you in this tapestry.

Now that you have a sense of the historical and cultural depth behind sexual transmutation, you're better equipped to appreciate the nuances of the techniques we'll cover. In the next chapters, we'll dive deeper into the **benefits** of sexual transmutation how it can supercharge creativity, foster emotional resilience, and ignite intimacy. We'll also explore the nitty-gritty of **how** to do it: the breathwork, the mindset, and the daily practices.

But before that, take a moment to reflect: Which historical approach intrigues you the most? How might it inform your personal journey? By connecting to a lineage of explorers, you honor the richness of this human endeavor and set the stage for your own mind-blowing, heart-expanding, soul-stirring *MINDGASM*.

CHAPTER 3

Influential Thinkers and Cultural Practices: From Renaissance Masters to Netflix-Era Gurus

Welcome to Chapter 3, where we'll spotlight a colorful cast of **influential figures**, **eccentric visionaries**, and **cultural icons** who, in one way or another, harnessed sexual energy to propel themselves or their societies to new heights. Along the way, we'll keep things cheeky and real, acknowledging the occasional comedic side of desire (yes, including "blue balls"), while gleaning wisdom that can inspire our own *mindgasmic* adventures.

3.1 Renaissance Rebels: Da Vinci, Michelangelo, and the Power of Artistic Obsession

Let's start in the era of dramatic art, plumed hats, and the heady swirl of new ideas. The **Renaissance** gave birth to many creative geniuses who seemed to have *endless* supplies of passion. Some historians speculate that these luminaries tapped into their sexual energies intentionally or not to feed their unstoppable drive.

1. Leonardo da Vinci

Known for painting the *Mona Lisa* and conceptualizing inventions centuries ahead of his time.

Rumors swirl about his personal life, with some suggesting he sublimated sexual desire into his **fervent curiosity** leading him to dissect corpses, design flying machines, and paint iconic masterpieces.

While we don't have a diary entry reading, "I transmuted my lust today to draw that helicopter," it's not a stretch to imagine that his deep well of creative energy was fueled by an inner passion that extended beyond mere intellect.

2. Michelangelo

The sculptor of *David*, painter of the Sistine Chapel, and notorious for being a bit of a loner.

Some scholars point to his intense devotion to art as a form of **sexual transmutation** channeling personal longing into the chiseled perfection of marble figures.

A few letters hint at a turbulent emotional life, possibly including unfulfilled romantic or sexual yearnings, which he poured into his craft instead of letting it idle.

Takeaway: Even if you're not painting chapel ceilings, you can adopt the Renaissance spirit by using your own yearnings romantic, sensual, or otherwise to **fuel** your projects. Next time you're eyeing that unstarted passion project, think of Michelangelo up on that scaffold, day after day, using every ounce of fervor to bring art to life.

3.2 The Scientific Romantics: Tesla, Edison, and the "Mad Scientist" Vibe

Moving forward in time, let's tip our hats to the Industrial Age where innovation soared, patents multiplied, and a new breed of "scientific romantics" emerged. Two iconic inventors come to mind: **Nikola Tesla** and **Thomas Edison**.

1. Nikola Tesla

Known for pioneering alternating current (AC) electricity, Tesla coils, and a head full of wild hair that matched his radical ideas.

Famously unmarried, Tesla claimed celibacy was crucial to his inventions. In modern terms, we might say he practiced a form of "sexual transmutation" funneling potential romantic or sexual energy into his groundbreaking research.

Did he ever experience "blue balls" from all that abstinence? Perhaps. But if so, he seems to have turned that tension into **lightning-bolt** inspiration literally.

2. Thomas Edison

The pragmatic counterpart to Tesla's flamboyant genius, Edison held over 1,000 patents, including the phonograph and practical electric light bulb.

Less is written about his personal sexual beliefs, but he spoke frequently about **energy, persistence**, and the "burning desire" to solve problems language that parallels the concept of harnessing primal drives.

Takeaway: You don't have to renounce dating apps or physical intimacy to emulate Tesla's focus. The lesson is that *any* surge of desire whether from flirting, daydreaming, or a random crush can be captured and converted into "inventive spark." If you find yourself feeling that *itch* (the one that might lead to a quick text to your ex), pause and consider: "Could I direct this surge into brainstorming for my next big idea?"

3.3 Modern Mystics and the Psychedelic Movement

Jumping to the mid-20th century, we encounter a wave of **spiritual explorers** and **psychedelic pioneers** who wove sexuality, creativity, and consciousness expansion into one kaleidoscopic tapestry.

1. Alan Watts

A British philosopher who popularized Eastern philosophy in the West.

While not strictly a "sexual transmutation guru," he often spoke about the unity of body and mind, hinting that sexual desire could be a path to **ecstatic awareness** if approached mindfully.

2. Timothy Leary and the "Turn On, Tune In, Drop Out" Era

Associated with LSD experiments, Leary's philosophy included exploring all forms of human consciousness, including sexual expression.

Though he didn't pen a how-to on transmutation per se, his call to "turn on" can be loosely interpreted as an invitation to harness life's energies sexual or otherwise to "tune in" to deeper truths.

3. Sexual Liberation Meets Spiritual Exploration

The '60s and '70s brought about freer attitudes toward sexuality, at least in some circles.

Workshops, communes, and spiritual retreats began to integrate sexual energy with meditation, yoga, and communal living, paving the way for more open discussion about channeling desire for personal growth.

Takeaway: While you don't need to drop acid or join a commune to explore your sexual energy, there's value in seeing how these modern mystics linked **openness**, **curiosity**, and **holistic living** to harness the full spectrum of human experience body, mind, and spirit.

3.4 Contemporary Pop Gurus: The Tony Robbins–Style Motivators

In the self-help and motivational circuit, you'll find a host of "pop gurus" who might not explicitly say "sexual transmutation," but they'll talk about **"turning your passion into results"** or **"fueling your unstoppable drive."** Figures like Tony Robbins, Brendon Burchard, and Marie Forleo often emphasize:

Emotional Intensity: They encourage you to get fired up, jump around, or shout affirmations. That intensity is akin to sexual energy a surge that, if harnessed, can break limiting beliefs and power up your ambition.

Peak State: These coaches teach you to condition your physiology (posture, breathing, movement) to tap into unstoppable confidence. Sexual arousal is a natural "peak state," so bridging that energy to your daily life can yield a similar unstoppable vibe.

Takeaway: Next time you watch a high-energy seminar, notice how the speaker revs you up. That hype is a cousin to the surge you feel when flirting or daydreaming about a crush. The difference? In the seminar, you're funneling that energy into *motivation* rather than *seduction*. Same principle, different direction.

3.5 Cultural Crossovers: K-Pop, Bollywood, and the Global Seduction

It's not just about Western gurus or Eastern mystics. In today's hyperconnected world, entire **pop culture** industries revolve around harnessing (and selling) sexual energy in a more mainstream way.

1. **K-Pop's Intense Fandom**

K-Pop stars often exude a polished, flirtatious aura that leaves fans swooning.

The fervor these artists ignite can be seen as a communal wave of sexual/creative energy. Some fans channel it into making fan art, writing fan fiction, or even learning Korean again, a form of transmutation.

2. **Bollywood's Dance and Romance**

Indian cinema is famous for elaborate dance numbers that ooze romance and longing, yet often remain (somewhat) "clean" by Western standards.

Viewers might feel a flutter of desire during these sequences, which can become creative fuel "I want to learn that dance!" or "I feel so energized, I'll try writing my own story!"

3. **Western Pop Icons**

From Beyoncé's empowering sexuality to Harry Styles' gender-blurring outfits, modern pop stars can harness sexual energy to shape cultural conversations.

Their fans often feed off that vibe, using it to fuel personal transformations, from adopting bolder fashion choices to pushing for social change.

Takeaway: You don't have to become a pop idol, but you can glean a lesson: sexual energy, when presented confidently, can galvanize large groups of people to create art, movements, and new cultural expressions.

3.6 "Blue Balls" and the Art of Frustration

Okay, let's address the *ache* in the room: **blue balls** (or for some folks, the equally uncomfortable pelvic congestion that doesn't discriminate by gender). It's that throbbing tension when you're aroused but don't get a physical release. Often joked about, sometimes cursed, but rarely seen as a potential tool.

1. Why It Happens

During arousal, blood flow increases in the pelvic region. If you're consistently "revved up" without release, you might feel an ache or mild pain.

For many, it's an annoyance. For others, it's a comedic punchline.

2. The Transmutation Spin

Instead of cursing your body, consider that physical tension a **reservoir** of energy.

Through breathwork or a quick physical movement (like dancing, stretching, or a cold shower if you're really in a pinch), you can redirect that tension upward toward your brain, your heart, your creativity.

3. Lighthearted Flirt and Tension

Ever been in a flirty situation that ends abruptly maybe your crush leaves, or the conversation shifts? You're left in a state of *unresolved excitement*. That's prime transmutation territory.

Next time you feel the "argh!" of unfulfilled desire, think: "Cool, I've got a half-charged battery here. Where can I plug it in?"

4. Caution and Comfort

If discomfort is severe or persistent, physical relief (solo or partnered) might be the best route. Transmutation shouldn't mean ignoring pain or pushing your body's limits in an unhealthy way.

The key is balance: harness what you can, but don't torture yourself. This is about empowerment, not masochism.

Cheeky Reminder: Sometimes a little frustration can be comedic like a comedic sidekick in a movie. But you can turn that comedic tension into a creative subplot for your own life. "Blue balls: the unexpected ally in finishing that novel or tackling that big work proposal." It's silly, but you get the idea.

3.7 Real Talk: The Role of Celebrity Sex Symbols

1. Marilyn Monroe, Elvis, Rihanna, etc.

These figures radiated (or radiate) sexual allure that fans either want to emulate or be near.

The tension they evoke can spark waves of creativity just look at how many songs, fan arts, or entire fashion lines are inspired by these icons.

2. Turning Idol Worship into Personal Power

Instead of pining after a celebrity or losing hours to daydreams, channel that *spark* into something you create. Maybe you write a short story featuring a character inspired by your celeb crush's confidence or style.

That's sexual transmutation in a pop-culture nutshell.

3. The Flip Side: Obsession

If you're spending all day fantasizing about your favorite star, that might lead to stagnation in your own life.

Recognize when your admiration crosses into unproductive obsession. If that line is blurred, use transmutation techniques (like breathwork or journaling) to pivot that energy into your personal goals.

3.8 From Cult Followings to Modern Coaching: The Rise of Sexual Empowerment Experts

In the last couple of decades, an entire cottage industry has sprung up around "sexual empowerment." You'll find:

1. Workshops and Retreats:

Ranging from mild (couples' communication courses) to wild (naked yoga, yoni worship, or tantric massage intensives).

Some are purely sensational, but many are grounded in legitimate techniques that echo ancient teachings, repackaged for modern audiences.

2. Online Courses and Webinars:

Some coaches (like Kim Anami, Layla Martin, or Jaiya) focus on "conscious sexuality" or "erotic intelligence."

They often incorporate transmutation principles, teaching how to cultivate sexual energy and direct it toward life goals.

3. "Lighthearted Flirt" as a Teaching Tool:

Many empowerment gurus use humor, playful banter, or provocative marketing to get your attention because let's face it, sex sells.

If you're drawn to a particular teacher's style, see if their approach aligns with your values and comfort level.

Takeaway: This realm can be a goldmine of knowledge but be discerning. Not every coach is legit, and some programs might be more about hype than substance. Look for those who emphasize **ethics**, **consent**, and **holistic well-being**.

3.9 A Lighthearted Flirt with the Future: VR, AI, and Beyond

What does sexual transmutation look like in the age of **virtual reality** (VR) and **artificial intelligence** (AI)? It might sound sci-fi, but these technologies are rapidly evolving.

1. VR Experiences

Some VR platforms offer immersive "adult" content that can evoke strong arousal. The question is: can that surge be directed into creative or emotional growth? Possibly.

Imagine finishing a VR session and then jumping into a brainstorming spree for your next invention still riding that wave of excitement.

2. AI Companions

With AI "chatbot girlfriends/boyfriends" on the rise, people may develop emotional or sexual attachments to digital entities.

If that emotional tension builds, a wise user could say, "Okay, I'm feeling that spark. Let me transmute it into finishing my coding project or writing my business plan."

3. **Ethical Considerations**

As technology blurs lines between reality and simulation, we must keep our moral compass intact. Sexual transmutation is about empowerment, not escapism to the point of neglecting real-world responsibilities or relationships.

Takeaway: The future is wild and full of new frontiers. The principle of harnessing sexual energy remains the same **awareness, direction, and intention**. Even in a VR-laden, AI-driven tomorrow, we'll still have bodies, minds, and desires that can be channeled productively.

3.10 Conclusion: Standing on the Shoulders of Giants (Who Might Have Been a Little Horny)

From Renaissance masters to Tesla's electric brilliance, from Tantric yogis to modern-day coaches and pop stars there's a common thread: **passion**. That passion might manifest as raw lust, unrequited longing, creative obsession, or spiritual fervor. The point is, when harnessed wisely, it can catapult individuals (and sometimes entire cultures) into new realms of possibility.

So, dear reader, let this chapter remind you that you're **not alone** in your pursuit of harnessing sexual energy. You're part of a vast lineage an ever-growing tapestry of people who realized that desire is more than a fleeting bodily impulse. It's a **cosmic spark**, a life-affirming force that can shape art, technology, spirituality, and personal transformation.

Now, with historical context and modern examples under your belt, you're better equipped to appreciate the next layers of *MINDGASM*. In Chapter 4, we'll dive into the **science** behind sexual energy exploring hormones, neuroscience, and how your body's physiology can either help or hinder your attempts at transmutation. Because yes, dear friend, it's time to see how your body's built-in chemistry can become your best ally in this journey. Let's go get scientific, shall we?

CHAPTER 4

The Science Behind Sexual Energy: Hormones, Brain Waves, and the Alchemy of Arousal

Buckle up, because in this chapter we're getting **nerdy** in the best way possible. Sexual transmutation might sound mystical or purely psychological, but there's a solid bedrock of **biology** and **neuroscience** that supports why this concept works. If you've ever wondered what's really happening under the hood when you feel that seductive pull or that unstoppable drive, read on.

4.1 Hormonal Orchestra: Testosterone, Estrogen, and Beyond

1. Testosterone

Commonly associated with masculinity, but present in all genders. It's a major driver of **libido**, **confidence**, and **assertiveness**.

When sexual arousal kicks in, testosterone can spike, leading to heightened focus and a willingness to **take risks**. Perfect for fueling that bold business pitch or launching your new art project.

2. Estrogen

Often tied to femininity, but again, all genders produce it in varying amounts.

Estrogen contributes to **mood regulation**, **skin health**, and even aspects of sexual desire.

Some research suggests balanced estrogen levels can enhance **creativity** and **emotional intelligence** key ingredients for empathetic leadership and innovation.

3. Progesterone

Typically overshadowed by estrogen and testosterone, but it plays a role in balancing the effects of both.

Fluctuations in progesterone can influence mood, energy, and overall sense of well-being. If you're feeling random bouts of irritability or lethargy, it might be your hormones nudging you to re-balance.

4. **Prolactin**

Often released post-orgasm, associated with **relaxation** and **satiety**.

If your goal is transmutation (rather than immediate release), you might delay or redirect orgasm to keep the tension and thus, the energy circulating for creative or professional tasks.

Cheeky Note: Don't worry, you won't have to pass a hormone exam to practice sexual transmutation. Just recognize that your body's chemistry is dynamic. If you ever feel those "blue balls" or a "pent-up" vibe, it's partially these hormones swirling around, looking for an outlet.

4.2 Neurochemical Bliss: Dopamine, Oxytocin, and Endorphins

1. **Dopamine: The "I Want It" Chemical**

Responsible for **motivation**, **reward**, and that "gotta have it" feeling whether it's a slice of pizza or a romantic fling.

When you're aroused, dopamine surges, making you more driven to pursue your "target." By consciously shifting that target (say, from a person to a creative project), you harness that same *oomph*.

2. **Oxytocin: The Cuddle Hormone**

Released during hugging, cuddling, and orgasm, it fosters **bonding** and trust.

If you're practicing partnered transmutation, building oxytocin can deepen emotional intimacy, making it easier to share goals and direct energy collectively.

3. **Endorphins: Natural Painkillers and Mood Boosters**

Kick in during exercise, laughter, or sexual activity, giving you that "feel-good" rush.

Endorphins can counter stress hormones (like cortisol), which is why a mild arousal can shift you from anxious to calm, especially when you direct that energy mindfully.

4. Serotonin: The Calm Satisfaction

While dopamine is about "wanting," serotonin is about **contentment** feeling stable and satisfied.

A balanced approach to sexual transmutation can help you maintain a healthy serotonin level, preventing the crash that sometimes follows an intense dopamine high.

Pro Tip: If you notice your mood or drive fluctuating wildly, it might be your neurochemistry at play. Tools like journaling, breathwork, or mindful movement can help regulate these chemicals, ensuring you stay in the sweet spot for transmutation.

4.3 Brain Waves: From Beta Bustle to Theta Thrills

1. Beta Waves (13–30 Hz)

Dominant when you're alert, focused, or problem-solving.

Mild sexual arousal can actually boost Beta waves, helping you concentrate. But too much tension might tip you into stress or anxious overthinking.

2. Alpha Waves (8–12 Hz)

Associated with relaxed wakefulness like a meditative or lightly daydreaming state.

A gentle flirt or a soft build of arousal can enhance alpha waves, providing a calm-yet-alert mental zone that's ideal for creative tasks.

3. Theta Waves (4–7 Hz)

Linked to deeper relaxation, dream states, and creativity. Some advanced practitioners of transmutation aim to hold sexual energy while dipping into **theta** a state that can spark visionary ideas or spiritual insights.

4. Gamma Waves (30+ Hz)

Often associated with peak concentration and sometimes mystical experiences.

A well-managed sexual charge can push you into a gamma-like "flow state," where time melts away, and you're fully immersed in the task at hand.

Takeaway: Sexual transmutation can be seen as a method to shift brain waves deliberately, from stressed-out Beta to a more creative Alpha or Theta zone. Next time you feel that tingle of desire, consider using a quick breath exercise to steer your mind into a more open, imaginative state.

4.4 Stress Hormones vs. Sexual Energy: Cortisol, Adrenaline, and the Balance Game

1. Cortisol: The Stress Bully

Elevated by deadlines, arguments, or that never-ending to-do list.

High cortisol can suppress sexual desire. Conversely, healthy sexual arousal can reduce cortisol. It's a two-way street.

By consciously transmuting sexual energy, you might help buffer stress. On the flip side, letting stress run rampant can kill your mojo.

2. Adrenaline: The "Fight or Flight" Jolt

Triggered by excitement or fear, adrenaline can amplify arousal. This is why some couples feel extra frisky after a scary movie or thrilling adventure.

Too much adrenaline can lead to anxiety or jitters, so the key is harnessing that edge without letting it devolve into panic.

3. Finding Homeostasis

The body craves balance. If you're chronically stressed, your ability to generate or enjoy sexual energy might plummet. If you're never stressed, you might not have the impetus to direct that energy anywhere.

Using breathwork or short meditative breaks can help you maintain that sweet spot where sexual energy thrives without being overshadowed by stress.

Lighthearted Flirt Tip: Next time you're about to watch a suspenseful Netflix show with your crush, be aware of that adrenaline spike. Instead of letting it vanish when the credits roll, see if you can redirect it maybe you'll find yourself finishing a mini painting or writing a short poem while still riding the after-buzz.

4.5 The Body's Electrical System: Subtle Energies and Biofields

1. Meridians (Chinese Medicine)

These are energy channels throughout the body. Sexual energy, often stored in the lower abdomen, can be moved along these meridians to other areas like the heart or brain.

Acupuncture and qigong practitioners focus on unblocking these channels for overall vitality.

2. Nadis (Yogic Tradition)

Similar concept to meridians, with key pathways like **ida, pingala**, and **sushumna**.

Sexual transmutation in yoga often involves guiding energy up the spine (sushumna) to the higher chakras.

3. Biofield Science

Emerging Western research looks at the electromagnetic fields around the human body. Some hypothesize that sexual arousal changes these fields, though it's still on the fringes of mainstream science.

Regardless, many holistic healers treat sexual energy as a "charge" that can be measured or felt by sensitive individuals.

Cheeky Note: If you're skeptical about invisible energy channels, think of them as metaphors or psychological frameworks. You don't have to see them literally to benefit from the practice of "moving energy" via breath, movement, or visualization.

4.6 Orgasms, Blue Balls, and the Chemistry of Release vs. Retention

1. Orgasmic Neurochemistry

Orgasm floods the brain with dopamine, oxytocin, and endorphins, creating a blissful afterglow.

Post-orgasm, **prolactin** often rises, which can induce a sense of "enough, I'm good," potentially dampening immediate creative drive or focus.

2. Retention for Transmutation

Some forms of transmutation suggest **delaying** orgasm or even practicing "non-ejaculatory" intimacy for those with male anatomy, preserving that tension to direct it elsewhere.

This can lead to comedic moments of near-release followed by a strategic pause. Yes, it might cause fleeting discomfort or "blue balls," but if harnessed skillfully, that tension can morph into a turbocharged brainstorming session or an unstoppable workout.

3. Finding Your Balance

Not everyone wants to or should practice orgasm retention. It can be tricky, physically and emotionally.

If it resonates with you, approach it gradually maybe just once in a while, see how you feel. If the tension is too intense or distracting, consider partial release or a gentler approach.

Flirt Alert: There's a certain thrill in playing with that edge, like a flirtatious conversation that never quite becomes explicit. It's the tension that fuels desire and likewise, it can fuel your next big creative or professional push.

4.7 The Placebo (and Nocebo) Effect: Mind Over Hormones

1. Belief Shapes Biology

If you believe sexual transmutation works, your body may produce the hormone/neurotransmitter cocktail conducive to success. This is the **placebo effect** in action mindset influencing physical response.

Conversely, if you believe you're "cursed with zero sex drive," you might inadvertently create that reality (the nocebo effect).

2. Harnessing Belief

Positive affirmations, journaling, or simple statements like "I am brimming with creative energy" can prime your nervous system to support transmutation.

Even if it feels cheesy, remember that the brain is *suggestible*. Repeated statements can shift your baseline attitudes.

3. Research Tidbit

Studies show that placebos can trigger dopamine release in the brain so if you can conjure a sense of confidence about your sexual energy, you might literally *produce* more drive or motivation.

4.8 Integrating Science into Your Practice

1. Track Your Rhythms

Notice when you're naturally more aroused time of day, phase of your menstrual cycle (if applicable), or stress levels. Use that data to schedule tasks requiring extra creativity or drive.

For instance, if you wake up feeling a mild sexual buzz, do 15 minutes of writing or brainstorming before you even get out of bed.

2. Leverage Pre-Existing Highs

If a flirty chat gets your heart racing, pivot to a quick burst of work or a short creative session right after.

Think of it like "ride the wave" before it subsides.

3. **Observe the Aftermath**

If you do release physically (orgasm), note your mental state afterward. Are you relaxed and open to calm tasks, or do you feel like napping? Plan your day accordingly.

If you choose to retain, watch how your focus or creativity might spike. But also watch for signs of frustration or "blue ball meltdown." If that meltdown is imminent, it might be time for a different approach.

4.9 Common Questions and Clarifications

1. **"Will practicing sexual transmutation mess up my hormones?"**

Generally, no. You're just channeling natural urges. If anything, you might become more in tune with your body's signals.

If you have underlying hormonal imbalances, consult a healthcare provider.

2. **"What if I'm on birth control or hormone therapy?"**

You can still practice transmutation. Your baseline hormone levels might differ, but the fundamental principle redirecting arousal remains valid.

3. **"Is it dangerous to skip orgasms repeatedly?"**

For most healthy individuals, occasional retention isn't harmful. But if you experience persistent discomfort, it's your body telling you to ease up. Balance is key.

4. **"Can sexual transmutation help with low libido?"**

Potentially, yes. By actively engaging with your desire (rather than ignoring or forcing it), you might reignite the flame. However, if libido issues stem from deeper medical or psychological factors, a professional opinion is wise.

Lighthearted Moment: If your best friend texts you, "I have the worst case of blue balls," you can now respond, "Dude, channel that tension into finishing your novel!" They might roll their eyes, but who knows you could be sowing the seeds of transmutation for them too.

4.10 Conclusion: Embrace the Science, Enjoy the Magic

If Chapters 1 and 2 gave you the philosophical and historical "why," this chapter gave you the "how" from a biological standpoint. Understanding hormones, neurochemicals, and brain waves helps demystify the process. It's not all woo-woo or intangible. Your body's *wired* to respond to sexual cues **and** it's wired to redirect those cues into other forms of drive.

As you move forward, keep this science in your back pocket. Notice how your body reacts when you get a little flirty or a tad aroused maybe your posture changes, your voice deepens or brightens, your mind sharpens. That's your body's **engine** revving. You get to decide if you'll peel out in a squeal of tires or channel that horsepower into building the life you desire.

In our next chapters, we'll explore the **practical benefits** of sexual transmutation how it can skyrocket your creativity, supercharge your productivity, and even improve your emotional well-being. Ready to ride the wave of possibility? Let's keep this *mindgasmic* journey rolling!

CHAPTER 5

Expanding Creativity and Productivity: Turning Desire into Your Muse

You're sitting at your desk, half-empty coffee cup in hand, the cursor blinking accusingly on a blank page. Sound familiar? We've all been there: the dreaded creative slump or productivity plateau. But here's a radical thought: what if that next surge of arousal the one triggered by a flirty text or a random daydream could catapult you into a **creative flow** so powerful you forget writer's block ever existed?

Welcome to the world where **sexual transmutation** meets your **creative genius** and **work ethic**. In this chapter, we'll explore how to harness that oh-so-familiar spark of desire to supercharge your **artistic pursuits**, **problem-solving**, and **everyday tasks**. Because let's face it: sometimes you just need a bit of "I'm so turned on right now" to fuel "I'm about to nail this project."

5.1 Sexual Energy & the Creative Flow State

Flow State 101: Psychologist Mihaly Csikszentmihalyi famously described "flow" as that magical zone where you're so absorbed in an activity that time warps and everything clicks. Painters, coders, and athletes alike chase this state because it's where brilliance often happens.

1. Arousal as a Primer

Mild sexual tension can sharpen your focus, akin to a mental "warm-up." Think of it like revving your car engine before a race. You're more alert, senses tingling, mind abuzz with possibilities.

If you redirect that energy like turning the steering wheel toward a creative task, you might slip into flow more easily.

2. Boosting Dopamine and "Crush Energy"

We've talked about dopamine in Chapter 4. Here's the gist: sexual arousal spikes dopamine, which also underpins **motivation** and **reward**.

Remember that "crush energy" from your teen years, when you'd suddenly rearrange your entire bedroom at 2 a.m. because you were too giddy to sleep? That's dopamine. Now, harness it for your next masterpiece.

3. Mindset Shift

Instead of seeing sexual thoughts as distractions, view them as **ignition fuel**. You're not ignoring them; you're inviting them to the party just steering them to the dance floor of creativity instead of the bedroom.

5.2 Overcoming Creative Blocks with Sexual Transmutation

We all know that dreaded creative block. Maybe your paintbrush hovers over the canvas with no inspiration, or your code editor stares blankly back at you. Cue sexual transmutation.

1. Micro-Burst Technique

Next time you're stuck, take a brief "desire break." Close your eyes and recall a recent flirtatious moment or conjure a sensual memory that gets your blood pumping.

Let that excitement build for 30 seconds. Then before you lose that heat snap back to your project. Write, paint, brainstorm, or code for a solid 5–10 minutes without pause. Rinse and repeat as needed.

2. Flirt with Your Project

This might sound goofy, but try mentally flirting with your creative endeavor. Talk to your manuscript or design like it's your crush. "Hey there, gorgeous storyline, how about we spice you up with a new plot twist?" The silliness can dissolve seriousness, letting ideas flow more freely.

3. Breathwork for Blocks

If you feel tension building in your chest or a certain *lower region* (hello, "blue ball" tension), use a quick breath technique. Inhale deeply, imagine that energy rising to your head, exhale slowly. This can re-route the frustration into clarity.

Pro Tip: Sometimes a little sexual frustration is comedic gold. If you're on the brink of "blue balls," you might as well laugh at the irony and say, "Alright, body, let's paint an abstract piece about *this* tension!" Humor can unlock a surprising wave of creativity.

5.3 Productivity Hacks: From Arousal to Accomplishment

Productivity isn't just about getting stuff done; it's about **doing it efficiently and joyfully.** Sexual transmutation can offer a natural "kick" that competes with caffeine without the jitters.

1. The Arousal-Pomodoro

The classic Pomodoro Technique has you work in 25-minute sprints with 5-minute breaks. Spice it up: if you feel a spark of arousal in your break, harness it. Let that excitement bubble, then jump into your next 25-minute sprint fueled by that energy.

It's like giving your brain a mini shot of espresso but from an internal source. *Zero dollars spent on fancy lattes!*

2. "Desire Trigger" Playlists

Some songs just exude sensual vibes. Make a playlist of tunes that evoke mild desire or confidence nothing too distracting, just enough to keep you in a lightly turned-on state.

As you tackle tasks, let that music keep your dopamine flowing. This trick merges the body's natural chemistry with the motivational power of music.

3. Rewarding Tasks with Flirt Breaks

If you have a friend or partner you enjoy flirting with (and it's mutually respectful), schedule micro "flirt breaks" after completing a chunk of work.

That flirty chat can raise your energy again just remember to pivot back to tasks, or you'll end up in a 3-hour text spree about future date nights. The key is using the energy surge, not getting lost in it.

5.4 Channeling Desire into Brainstorming & Problem-Solving

1. The "Hot" Brainstorm

Gather your team or do a solo brainstorming session. Begin by recalling a moment that made your heart race like a near-kiss scene from a rom-com. Keep it PG enough for the workplace, but let that memory bring a blush to your cheeks.

Immediately dive into listing ideas or solutions. Notice how your adrenaline (and mild arousal) can remove inhibitions, allowing wilder, more creative ideas to surface.

2. Turning Lust into Lateral Thinking

Lateral thinking requires stepping out of conventional patterns. Sexual desire inherently shifts your mindset, focusing you on possibility.

If you can detach it from a purely physical outlet, you can apply that same sense of possibility to tricky puzzles, riddles, or business conundrums.

3. Solo "Sensual Solutions"

Next time you can't solve a problem like how to fix a leaky faucet or reorganize your living room allow a brief flush of desire. Let your mind wander to a fantasy or a real memory for a minute or two, then come back to the problem.

You might find a creative angle or an "aha!" moment that eluded you before.

5.5 Real-Life Anecdotes: From Office Crushes to Art Studios

1. Office Crush Productivity

Case: Dev, a marketing coordinator, had a serious crush on a colleague. Instead of letting it distract him all day, Dev decided to transmute that energy. Whenever he'd see his crush in the breakroom, he'd let himself feel that surge of excitement. Then he'd march back to his desk and tackle his campaign proposals with renewed vigor. Over a month, his metrics soared and his boss was none the wiser about his "secret sauce."

2. Art Studio Shenanigans

Case: Lila, an aspiring sculptor, found she produced her best work after a heated texting session with her long-distance partner. She'd let the "I miss you, can't wait to see you" vibes swirl inside her, then channel them into shaping clay with a fervor she never had before. Her pieces took on a dynamic, almost electric quality that galleries started to notice.

3. "Blue Balls" as a Comic Muse

Case: Jake, a stand-up comedian, joked onstage about being perpetually single and dealing with "chronic blue balls." But in private, he discovered that if he paused that tension didn't run to fix it physically he could write new bits with an edgy, raw humor. His comedic sets gained a spark that landed him a feature spot at a local comedy festival.

Lesson: The moral across these stories? A little unspent or mildly stoked sexual energy can be a *game-changer* when directed at your tasks. Whether you're analyzing data or molding clay, that tension and excitement can inject life into your work.

5.6 Practical Exercises: Harnessing Sexual Energy for Creativity & Productivity

Exercise 1: The Arousal-to-Action Switch

1. **Step 1**: Identify a mild arousal trigger maybe a memory of a steamy scene from a favorite show.
2. **Step 2**: Let the feeling build for 15–30 seconds. Don't go too far just enough to feel the warmth or tingles.

3. **Step 3**: Immediately switch to a focused task. Set a timer for 10 minutes, and work without interruption.
4. **Step 4**: After the timer, note how you felt. Did you produce more ideas? Move faster? If yes, great. If not, tweak your approach (maybe a different trigger or a different task).

Exercise 2: Sensual Brain Dump

- **Step 1**: Put on soft, atmospheric music something that stirs a sense of allure.
- **Step 2**: Lightly recall a moment of flirtation or an attractive person who makes you grin.
- **Step 3**: Brain dump all your project ideas, to-dos, or creative concepts onto paper for 5 minutes. No censoring!
- **Step 4**: Review your notes. Circle any gems that stand out. You might find your ideas are bolder or more playful than usual.

Exercise 3: Micro-Tingle Technique for Problem-Solving

- **Step 1**: Define the problem e.g., "How do I reorganize my living room for better flow?"
- **Step 2**: Inhale deeply, imagining a swirl of warm, tingly energy in your abdomen. If it helps, recall a brief, pleasant daydream.
- **Step 3**: Exhale, mentally directing that energy to your mind's eye.
- **Step 4**: Rapidly brainstorm 3–5 solutions. Even if they sound silly, list them.
- **Step 5**: Check if any solution resonates more strongly now that you're riding that mild wave of arousal.

5.7 Embrace the Playful Edge

Sexual energy in the realm of creativity and productivity doesn't have to be stiff or clinical pun absolutely intended. It can be playful, cheeky, and even comedic. Think of it as a personal superpower you can flick on whenever you need a dash of magic.

Lighthearted Flirt: Tease your tasks like they're your crush. Let that dynamic keep your mind engaged.

Blue Balls Humor: If you're feeling that pent-up tension, laugh about it. Let the comedic irony lighten your mood, then funnel the tension into your next painting, code snippet, or business pitch.

Self-Awareness: Recognize your thresholds. If the tension becomes distracting or frustrating, you might need a break or a gentle release this isn't about punishing yourself.

Key Takeaway: Creativity thrives on energy, novelty, and a willingness to explore. Sexual desire is a prime candidate for fueling all three. So next time you're stuck or bored, remember: a small spark of arousal might be exactly what your brain needs to leap into new territory.

CHAPTER 6

Emotional Resilience, Confidence, and Well-Being: Building Your Inner Fortress with Sexual Transmutation

So far, we've looked at harnessing sexual energy for creative sparks and productivity. But what about your emotional world your sense of **confidence, resilience,** and **overall well-being**? Believe it or not, sexual transmutation can also help you stand tall in the face of life's challenges, infusing you with a steady sense of self-worth and emotional equilibrium.

Let's dive into how redirecting desire can bolster your **mental health, emotional stability,** and **personal confidence** because a *mindgasm* isn't just about bright ideas or bigger paychecks; it's about feeling genuinely **awesome** in your own skin.

6.1 Sexual Energy & Emotional Health: A Surprising Connection

1. Hormones Meet Emotions

Recall from Chapter 4 how hormones like **oxytocin** and **dopamine** can uplift your mood. When you transmute sexual energy, you're playing with those chemicals in a conscious way.

Think of it as a gentle self-medication without the side effects where you use arousal to release tension and boost positivity.

2. Confidence Through Self-Trust

When you realize you can handle your own desires (rather than being ruled by them), your sense of self-trust soars.

This self-trust translates to confidence in other areas: if you can navigate the potent force of sexual energy, a challenging meeting or social event might feel like child's play.

3. Emotional Resilience

Life will throw curveballs stress at work, family drama, heartbreak. By learning to channel intense feelings (like sexual desire), you gain a blueprint for channeling other intense emotions.

The skill of "I feel something big let me redirect it productively" becomes a superpower for everything from anger to sadness.

6.2 Building Self-Esteem with Sexual Transmutation

Self-esteem often ties to how we perceive our worth, attractiveness, and capability. Sexual transmutation can give you a fresh lens on each of these.

1. Reframing Your Desires

Instead of labeling your urges as "lustful" or "inappropriate," view them as **life force** evidence that you're vibrant and alive.

This shift can dissolve guilt or shame, boosting self-esteem. After all, it's pretty cool to have an internal power source on tap.

2. Using Arousal to Combat Negative Self-Talk

The next time you catch yourself thinking, "I'm not good enough," do a quick breathwork exercise. Let a mild wave of desire remind you of your inherent power.

Pair that feeling with an affirmation: "I'm a creative, confident being." This duo arousal + affirmation can override negative loops.

3. Celebrating Body Positivity

Sexual energy thrives on body awareness. As you practice transmutation, you become more attuned to your body's signals and sensations.

This heightened body awareness can foster appreciation for your physique, even if it's not "perfect" by societal standards. You start seeing your body as an ally, not an adversary.

6.3 Emotional Resilience in Practice: From "Blue Balls" to Breakups

1. "Blue Balls" Turned Zen

When that tension is building with no immediate relief, you have a choice: frustration or transmutation. By choosing the latter, you learn that you can endure and even harness discomfort.

This small act of resilience managing physical tension translates into greater mental toughness for life's bigger stressors.

2. Channeling Heartbreak

Post-breakup, sexual desire might still linger or flare up unpredictably. Instead of letting it spiral into self-pity, you can transmute that energy into a new passion learning an instrument, volunteering, starting a side hustle.

Over time, this practice helps you see heartbreak as a catalyst for growth rather than a pit of despair.

3. Stress Overload

Big deadlines or personal crises can lead to suppressed libido or chaotic desire swings. By consciously tapping into any flicker of arousal and redirecting it, you create pockets of emotional relief.

• The sense of control gained here fosters resilience, reminding you that you can steer your internal states even in stormy weather.

6.4 Confidence Amplifiers: How Sexual Transmutation Boosts Self-Assuredness

1. Embodied Confidence

When you carry sexual energy in a conscious way, your posture changes spine a bit straighter, walk a bit more purposeful. People notice.

This physical presence often begets social and professional confidence, creating a positive feedback loop.

2. Mental Clarity

Sexual tension, when left unchanneled, can cloud your thoughts (cue daydreaming about the barista's smile). But if you harness it, you gain clarity of purpose.

That clarity radiates as confidence knowing exactly what you want and going for it without hesitation.

3. Risk-Taking Edge

Mild arousal can embolden you to step outside your comfort zone. Maybe you pitch a bold idea at work or finally ask out that crush.

Each time you act on that courage, your confidence grows, reinforcing the cycle.

Comedic Perspective: Ever been in a flirty situation that gave you the "I can do anything" vibe? That's the gist. Sexual energy can transform you from "eh, maybe next time" to "heck yes, let's do this!"

6.5 Self-Care and Well-Being: Beyond the Bedroom

1. Holistic Health

Research suggests healthy sexual expression correlates with better cardiovascular health, lower stress, and improved mood. Transmutation extends that "healthy sexuality" into daily life.

If you're using sexual energy to fuel exercise, creative hobbies, or mindful meditation, you're effectively doubling down on well-being.

2. Balancing Release and Retention

Sometimes you just need to let go (physically). Other times, you retain the tension for transmutation. Finding your personal balance is key to overall wellness.

If you're constantly retaining and feeling cranky, that's not well-being. If you're constantly releasing, you might miss the benefits of harnessing tension. Experiment to find your sweet spot.

3. Emotional Literacy

Transmutation requires awareness of your emotional states. "Am I anxious, bored, or actually aroused?" Distinguishing these can reduce emotional eating, impulsive shopping, or other coping mechanisms.

Over time, you become more adept at naming and navigating emotions a cornerstone of mental health.

6.6 Real-Life Anecdotes: Transforming Emotional Turmoil into Strength

1. Anxiety to Assurance

Case: Priya, who struggled with social anxiety, discovered that if she lightly engaged with a memory of her partner's affectionate touch before entering a social event, her jitters subsided. She felt a subtle wave of warmth and confidence that replaced the knot in her stomach. Over months, her social skills blossomed.

2. From "Blue Ball" Stress to Calm Composure

Case: Damon often ended up with unfulfilled arousal after late-night texting sessions with his LDR partner. Instead of stewing in frustration, he'd do a short yoga flow, channeling that tension into mindful movement. The result? He felt relaxed, proud of his discipline, and less anxious about the distance in his relationship.

3. Breakup Rebirth

Case: Tasha went through a rough breakup, feeling both heartache and random surges of longing. She poured that longing into daily journaling and a new painting series. As the weeks passed, her art gained depth, and her emotional wounds gradually healed. She credits sexual transmutation for turning her sorrow into a creative renaissance.

6.7 Practical Exercises: Building Emotional Resilience & Confidence

Exercise 1: The Desire-Dial Check-In

- **Step 1**: Visualize a dial from 0 (no desire) to 10 (intense desire).

- **Step 2**: Ask yourself, "Where am I on this dial right now?" If it's above a 3, see if you can channel that into a small action like journaling a quick gratitude list or setting a tiny goal.
- **Step 3**: If you're at a 7+ but can't release physically, do 10 slow breaths, imagining the tension flowing up to your heart. Let it fuel a sense of warmth and self-love.

Exercise 2: Affirmations Under Mild Arousal

- **Step 1**: Recall a flirty or sensual memory that gently arouses you (aim for a 3–5 on the dial).
- **Step 2**: Speak or think affirmations like:

    "I am strong and capable."

    "My desires fuel my growth."

    "I welcome abundance and creativity."

- **Step 3**: Feel how the mild arousal intensifies these affirmations. Journal any shifts in your emotional state.

Exercise 3: Emotional Re-Route

- **Step 1**: Identify a negative emotion stress, anger, sadness. Rate its intensity on a 0–10 scale.
- **Step 2**: Consciously tap into a memory or fantasy that sparks mild arousal. Breathe it in.
- **Step 3**: On the exhale, imagine the negative emotion loosening, making space for a new sense of empowerment.
- **Step 4**: Repeat a few cycles. Notice if the negative emotion's intensity drops.

6.8 Navigating Emotional Intimacy and Boundaries

1. Sharing with a Partner

If you're in a relationship, consider communicating about using sexual energy to boost confidence or emotional resilience. It can be a bonding conversation.

But remember, not everyone is comfortable discussing sexual topics in detail. Respect boundaries.

2. Respecting Your Own Limits

If certain fantasies or triggers feel overwhelming, scale back. Emotional health thrives on feeling safe, not forced.

Seek therapy or counseling if deeper issues (like past trauma) surface. Sexual transmutation is a tool, not a magic cure.

3. Community Support

Online forums or local workshops on mindful sexuality might provide camaraderie. Hearing others' stories can normalize your journey.

However, always keep personal safety and comfort in mind. Share only what feels right.

6.9 Embrace the Cheeky Side for Emotional Well-Being

Let's be real: part of building resilience is learning to **laugh** at life's absurdities. Sexual energy can be comedic. Think about it: the human body can be awkward, "blue balls" can be comedic frustration, and random daydreams can strike at inopportune moments. Embrace the silliness. Let it lighten your emotional load.

Flirt with Life: Instead of flirting only with people, flirt with experiences. Let curiosity and playful energy color your approach to daily tasks.

Comedy of Tension: If you're stuck in traffic and you feel tension (sexual or otherwise), joke to yourself: "If I can handle blue balls, I can handle this jam." Humor is a potent emotional buffer.

6.10 Conclusion: Standing Tall in Every Storm

Sexual transmutation isn't just about cranking out creative work or building an empire; it's also about **inner peace** and **emotional fortitude**. By consciously channeling your arousal, you cultivate resilience, boost self-esteem, and foster a deep-seated confidence that radiates into all areas of life.

You're Stronger Than You Think: Every time you redirect desire into something constructive, you reinforce the belief that you can handle intense emotions.

Embrace the Joy: Let the playful side of sexual energy remind you that life can be fun, even in stressful times.

Stay Tuned: In upcoming chapters, we'll delve into relationships, spirituality, and advanced techniques, further broadening how sexual transmutation can transform your life from the inside out.

Now that you see how sexual energy can bolster your emotional well-being, get ready to deepen your understanding of relationships and intimacy in the next chapters. After all, a *mindgasm* is even more profound when shared or integrated into your spiritual path. Let's keep this journey rolling!

CHAPTER 7

Relationship Harmony and Intimacy: Transmuting Desire for Deeper Connections

In previous chapters, we explored how sexual energy can supercharge your creativity, productivity, and emotional well-being. But what about **love**? What about those shared moments ranging from playful flirtation to soul-baring vulnerability that define our most meaningful relationships?

This chapter dives into how **sexual transmutation** can enrich your romantic bonds, strengthen communication, and spice up intimacy. Whether you're in a long-term partnership, dating around, or flying solo (with future relationships in mind), these insights can help you harness sexual energy as a **connective force** not just a personal one.

7.1 The Essence of Relationship Harmony

1. Shared Energy, Shared Growth

When you're in a romantic relationship, your energies intersect. Sexual transmutation becomes a **team sport**, where both partners can channel desire into mutual goals be it traveling together, buying a home, or supporting each other's careers.

Picture desire as a communal piggy bank of vitality. Each partner contributes, and both reap the benefits.

2. Deepening Emotional Intimacy

Sexual desire often opens the door to vulnerability. By intentionally transmuting that energy, you can foster deeper **emotional closeness**. It's like using arousal as the glue that binds hearts, not just bodies.

Imagine lying together, hearts racing, but instead of rushing to release tension physically, you let that tension fuel a heartfelt conversation or a joint meditation.

3. Conflict Resolution

Tension in relationships isn't always sexual sometimes it's disagreement or resentment. However, the skill of redirecting intense feelings (like sexual energy) can also help you **transform** anger or frustration into constructive dialogue.

If you can master "I'm aroused but I'll channel this tension," you can also master "I'm upset but I'll channel this emotion into problem-solving."

7.2 From Flirty Beginnings to Lasting Connection

1. Early Dating and the "Spark"

In new relationships, sexual energy often surges think of those early flutters, sweaty palms, the "can't-stop-thinking-about-you" stage.

Transmuting that energy can help you keep a level head and **avoid love-blind mistakes**. For instance, you might funnel the excitement into thoughtful gestures or deeper conversations, rather than purely physical acts.

2. Building Trust Through Transparency

If you're exploring sexual transmutation, consider discussing it (lightly) with a new partner. "Hey, sometimes I like to channel my desire into creative stuff like cooking you a surprise dinner!" This can be a quirky but endearing conversation starter.

Honesty fosters **trust**. Even if your partner finds it odd at first, they might appreciate your self-awareness and emotional maturity.

3. Keeping the Flame Alive

Over time, the initial sizzle can fade if left unattended. Using sexual transmutation techniques like breathwork or mindful intimacy helps you **reignite** the spark, ensuring it's not just routine sex but a continuous journey of exploration.

Lighthearted Flirt: You can treat each date as an opportunity to channel that flirty energy into discovering new hobbies, planning spontaneous getaways, or surprising each other with creative date ideas. Sexual tension becomes the engine that drives relational adventures.

7.3 Sexual Energy as a Communication Tool

1. Non-Verbal Cues

Sexual desire heightens your awareness of **body language** eye contact, touch, posture. By staying mindful, you can sense when your partner is open or hesitant.

Transmutation means using that heightened awareness to improve communication. Maybe you notice your partner's shoulders tense, so you pivot to reassurance rather than pressing an argument.

2. Verbal Intimacy

The same surge of energy that fuels sweet talk in the bedroom can be redirected to **courageous conversations**. Feeling that spark can embolden you to share deeper feelings, apologize sincerely, or express gratitude more openly.

If you catch a wave of desire, consider harnessing it for a heartfelt "I appreciate you because..." talk. It might feel vulnerable, but that's where true intimacy thrives.

3. Conflict Resolution Revisited

Sometimes couples misdirect sexual frustration into fights or passive aggression. Recognize that pattern: "Am I picking a fight because I'm actually feeling sexual tension that's unmet?"

If so, name it. "Hey, I realize I'm feeling antsy. Let's either address our intimacy or channel this tension into something fun or productive together."

Cheeky Perspective: Next time you're about to bicker over who left the dishes in the sink, pause. Ask yourself: "Am I just frustrated because we haven't had a good cuddle in a while?" Sometimes the tension is more *horizontal* than household chores.

7.4 Partnered Transmutation Techniques

Technique 1: Syncing Breath for Shared Intent

- **Sit Facing Each Other**: Close your eyes or maintain soft eye contact.
- **Inhale Together**: Visualize sexual energy pooling in your lower abdomen.
- **Exhale Together**: Imagine sending that energy up to your hearts, linking them in a shared circuit.
- **Verbalize a Joint Goal**: Whisper or speak a mutual aspiration like "We channel this energy into building our dream home" or "We direct this warmth into deeper understanding."

Technique 2: Sensual Touch Without Immediate Release

- **Light Touch**: Explore each other's bodies gently, focusing on sensation rather than escalation.
- **Pause Often**: When arousal spikes, pause and breathe together. Feel the tension. Instead of seeking release, let it simmer.
- **Mutual Visualization**: Each partner pictures the energy fueling a relationship goal or personal ambition. This can be deeply bonding, reminding you both that desire is a **team resource**.

Technique 3: The Post-Intimacy Redirection

- **Afterglow Awareness**: Post-sex or post-cuddle, you're relaxed. Instead of drifting off, share a moment of gratitude or talk about something you want to achieve as a couple.
- **Oxytocin Flow**: That cuddle hormone fosters trust. Use it to deepen emotional conversation maybe plan a future trip or discuss a shared dream.
- **Gentle Commitment**: Affirm you'll both channel the positive energy you feel right now into the rest of your day or week.

7.5 Navigating Different Desires and Boundaries

1. Mismatched Libidos

One partner might have a higher drive than the other. Sexual transmutation can help the higher-drive partner channel some of that surplus into personal pursuits, reducing pressure on the lower-drive partner.

Meanwhile, the lower-drive partner might explore gentle ways to stoke desire or share in transmutation exercises at a comfortable pace.

2. Consent and Comfort

Always remember that sexual transmutation is an **internal** process. You're not forcing your partner to do anything they're uncomfortable with.

If you want to share specific techniques (like breath sync), ensure both parties agree. No one should feel coerced or "guilted" into it.

3. Open Communication

If your partner doesn't vibe with the concept of transmutation, that's okay. You can still practice solo. Or you can find small aspects they might enjoy, like breathwork or mindful touch.

Keep the dialogue open, respectful, and non-judgmental.

7.6 Humor, "Blue Balls," and Relational Bonds

1. Laughing at Tension

If you're both feeling "hot and bothered" but choose to hold off on release, it can become comedic. Acknowledge the silliness: "We're basically two volcanoes, about to blow, but let's see if we can channel this to plan our next vacation!"

Shared laughter over sexual tension can strengthen emotional bonds, transforming frustration into a playful memory.

2. Turning Frustration into Teasing

Gentle teasing can be a form of flirtation. "I see that look in your eye. Are we going to direct that into finishing the yard work first?" This interplay can lighten the mood and remind both partners that desire is a resource, not a chore.

3. Celebrating Release

Of course, if you do opt for physical release together, you can appreciate it even more, knowing you sometimes hold off to channel energy. The variety retention sometimes, release other times keeps intimacy fresh.

7.7 Real-Life Stories: Couples Who Transmute Together

1. Alyssa & Marco

Married for 10 years, they felt the spark fading. After discovering transmutation, they tried the "syncing breath" technique once a week. They reported feeling more **emotionally connected**, and their arguments decreased because they channeled tension into these sessions instead of letting it fester.

2. Sam & Tori

In a new relationship with high sexual chemistry, they worried about moving too fast physically. By practicing occasional "pause-and-breathe" moments during intimacy, they built deeper trust. Tori said, "It was so romantic. Instead of rushing, we let desire intensify our emotional bond."

3. Leon & Jacob

A same-sex couple who used transmutation to manage stress from demanding careers. They'd come home, do a quick breath sync, and redirect any sexual tension into brainstorming solutions for their business. Over six months, their startup took off, and they credit that synergy to harnessing desire as motivation.

7.8 Practical Exercises: Relationship Harmony & Intimacy

Exercise 1: Pre-Date Energy Tune-Up

- **Step 1**: Before a date (or quality time at home), spend 2 minutes recalling a memory of your partner that makes you tingle maybe a favorite kiss or a sweet moment.
- **Step 2**: Breathe that feeling upward, imagining it filling your chest.

- **Step 3**: Go into the date with a warm, open vibe, ready to share that energy through genuine conversation or affectionate touch.

Exercise 2: The "Two Hearts, One Goal" Visualization

- **Step 1**: Sit together, holding hands. Close your eyes.
- **Step 2**: Each partner silently identifies one personal goal.
- **Step 3**: Inhale, feeling desire for each other. Exhale, imagining that combined desire fueling each partner's goal.
- **Step 4**: Share your goals aloud if comfortable, reaffirming mutual support.

Exercise 3: Post-Argument Reset

- **Step 1**: If you've had a tense argument, find a quiet moment.
- **Step 2**: Acknowledge any lingering sexual tension or emotional energy.
- **Step 3**: Decide together if you want to channel that tension into a collaborative task (cleaning up, cooking a meal, journaling side by side).
- **Step 4**: Reflect afterward on how it felt to transmute conflict into productive action or gentle intimacy.

7.9 Conclusion: Love, Lust, and Lasting Harmony

Relationships can be a **beautiful dance** of energies. Sexual transmutation is like learning a special choreography where you and your partner direct your combined desire not just into fleeting pleasure, but into **deepening love**, **shared ambitions**, and **harmonious growth**.

Embrace Teamwork: You're in this together, whether you're newly dating or long-term committed.

Celebrate the Tension: A little sexual frustration can be comedic and bonding just handle it with mutual respect.

Keep Communicating: Be honest about what works, what feels silly, and what feels amazing.

Next up, we'll explore the **spiritual** dimensions of sexual transmutation, because sometimes that spark in your loins can lead to a spark in your **soul**. Ready to ascend to new heights? Let's go!

CHAPTER 8

Spiritual Growth and Higher Consciousness: Ascending Beyond the Physical

So far, we've focused on the tangible perks of sexual transmutation productivity, creativity, emotional well-being, relationship harmony. But for many, there's a **deeper** call: the sense that sexual energy can be a **gateway** to profound spiritual experiences or even transcendent states of consciousness.

In this chapter, we'll explore how redirecting your primal desire can lead to **heightened awareness**, **inner peace**, and a feeling of **cosmic connection**. Whether you identify as religious, spiritual-but-not-religious, or simply curious, these insights can open new doors to your *mindgasmic* journey.

8.1 The Intersection of Sexuality and Spirituality

1. A Universal Thread

From Tantric practices in India to Christian mystics in medieval Europe, countless traditions have recognized a link between **sexual desire** and **divine union.**

Sexual energy is often described as the **most potent** form of human vitality so potent, it can break open the doors to higher realms if channeled consciously.

2. Ego Dissolution

Intense sexual desire or orgasm can momentarily silence the chatter of the ego, revealing a glimpse of unity or oneness.

By learning to hold and transmute that desire, you can **extend** that sense of unity, merging physical ecstasy with spiritual insight.

3. Sacredness in Everyday Life

You don't have to be in a temple or on a meditation cushion to feel spiritual. The act of acknowledging your own sexual energy as "sacred life force" can turn **everyday moments** into opportunities for reverence.

8.2 Kundalini Awakening and Chakra Alignment

1. Kundalini Basics

In yogic traditions, **Kundalini** is depicted as a coiled serpent at the base of the spine. When awakened, it travels upward through the chakras, leading to enlightenment or heightened consciousness.

Sexual desire is often a **key** to stirring this serpent, as it's intimately tied to the **root** (muladhara) and **sacral** (svadhisthana) chakras.

2. Chakra System

The body is said to have seven main chakras energy centers from the base of the spine to the crown of the head.

By channeling sexual energy up through these chakras, you can address emotional wounds, unlock creativity, open your heart, and expand your intuition.

3. Precautions

A full-on Kundalini awakening can be intense. Some experience physical tremors, emotional catharsis, or dramatic life changes.

Approach with respect. If you feel overwhelmed, grounding exercises (like walking barefoot, eating hearty meals) or professional guidance can help.

Cheeky Note: Think of Kundalini as that "holy wow" factor inside you. Tickle it gently. You don't want to poke the serpent too hard unless you're ready for a wild ride!

8.3 Tantra Beyond the Bedroom: The Cosmic Union

1. Tantric Philosophy

At its core, Tantra sees all reality as an interplay of **masculine** (Shiva) and **feminine** (Shakti) energies. Sexual union symbolizes cosmic union.

True Tantra isn't just about marathon intimacy sessions. It's a **life path** of mindfulness, devotion, and recognizing the sacred in all experiences.

2. Solo Tantric Exploration

You can practice Tantra solo by meditating on your **inner masculine and feminine** aspects.

During moments of arousal, visualize these energies dancing within you, merging in a radiant field of unity. This can lead to states of bliss or profound self-acceptance.

3. Partnered Tantra

If you have a willing partner, Tantric rituals might include eye-gazing, synchronized breathing, and prolonged, mindful intimacy.

The goal isn't orgasm; it's **oneness** letting sexual energy dissolve the illusion of separateness. When done respectfully, it can be an otherworldly experience.

8.4 Mystical Experiences and "Mindgasmic" States

1. Brain Wave Shifts

We discussed in Chapter 4 how sexual arousal can move you from Beta to Alpha or even Theta waves. In spiritual practice, Theta or Gamma waves often correlate with **mystical** experiences like deep meditation or trance states.

Arousal can catalyze these shifts faster than standard meditation, offering a **shortcut** to transcendent states if approached with intention.

2. Ego-Transcendence

Some practitioners describe moments during transmutation where the sense of "I" blurs, replaced by a feeling of **universal unity** or cosmic love.

This can be fleeting or life-altering, akin to a near-mystical revelation. While not guaranteed, it's a known phenomenon among those who combine sexuality with deep spiritual practice.

3. Body as Temple

Embracing your sexual energy spiritually means viewing your body as a **temple** a sacred vessel for divine energy.

This perspective can reduce body shame and foster reverence for every curve, scar, or quirk.

Comedic Perspective: If you ever find yourself thinking, "Did I just see God in the middle of a steamy breath session?" well, maybe you did! The lines between the physical and the divine can blur in the most unexpected ways.

8.5 Practical Techniques for Spiritual Transmutation

Technique 1: Heart-Crown Circuit

1. **Preparation**: Sit in a comfortable position, spine straight.
2. **Focus**: Gently stoke mild arousal (think of a sweet memory or a fantasy at a 3–4 intensity).
3. **Breath Path**: Inhale, visualizing the energy rising from your lower abdomen to your heart (anahata chakra). Exhale, sending it up to your crown (sahasrara chakra).
4. **Mantra (Optional)**: Repeat a phrase like "I unite body and spirit" or a sacred syllable (e.g., "Om").
5. **Integration**: Sit quietly afterward, noting any warmth, tingles, or expanded awareness.

Technique 2: The Sacred Self-Touch

1. **Atmosphere**: Dim lights, play soft music, and light a candle.
2. **Gentle Touch**: Instead of aiming for orgasm, explore your body slowly, focusing on sensations of warmth and energy flow.
3. **Visualization**: Each time you feel a surge, imagine it illuminating your spine like a column of light.

4.   **Completion**: End with a short prayer or affirmation, thanking your body for its capacity to experience pleasure and unity.

Technique 3: Devotional Eye-Gazing (Partnered)

1.   **Setup**: Sit facing each other, possibly in a dimly lit space.
2.   **Gaze**: Maintain soft eye contact, letting any sexual tension arise naturally.
3.   **Shared Mantra**: Together, chant a mantra or simply breathe in sync.
4.   **Sense of Oneness**: As desire grows, hold off on physical release. Focus on the sense of merging energies through the eyes. Some couples describe feeling like they can "see each other's souls."

8.6 Integrating Spiritual Practice into Daily Life

1. Morning Ritual

Start the day with 5 minutes of breathwork, gently acknowledging any sexual stirrings and directing them toward gratitude or universal love.

This sets a calm, centered tone like a mini spiritual tune-up.

2. Micro-Transmutation Moments

If you feel a spark of desire midday (maybe you see an attractive person on your lunch break), do a quick mental pivot: "I feel that warmth let me connect it to my heart and send out goodwill to the world."

It sounds whimsical, but it's a practice of turning personal desire into universal compassion.

3. Evening Reflection

Before bed, journal about moments when sexual energy surfaced. Did you transmute it for creativity, or did you hold it in a spiritual frame? How did it affect your mood or sense of connection?

Over time, patterns emerge, showing you how sexuality can become a consistent source of **inner peace** rather than mere fleeting pleasure.

8.7 Common Pitfalls and Myths About Spiritual Sexuality

1. **Myth**: "You Must Be Celibate to Be Spiritual."

Many traditions do emphasize celibacy, but plenty of others see sexual union as sacred. You can be spiritually vibrant whether you're celibate or actively intimate. The key is **mindful** practice, not avoidance.

2. **Myth**: "If I Practice Spiritual Transmutation, I'll Never Want Normal Sex Again."

Not true. You can absolutely enjoy physical release. In fact, spiritual awareness might make sex more meaningful and pleasurable, as you're bringing deeper presence to the experience.

3. **Pitfall**: "Spiritual Bypass"

Some folks try to use spiritual sexual practices to avoid emotional or psychological issues. True growth involves facing those issues, not ignoring them behind a veil of "I'm so enlightened."

Seek therapy or counseling if deeper traumas surface. Spiritual transmutation can complement professional help but isn't a one-stop cure.

4. **Pitfall**: "Cultish Dynamics"

Beware of groups or gurus who misuse sexual practices for manipulation. A legitimate spiritual practice respects **consent**, **autonomy**, and **safety**. If something feels off, trust your gut.

8.8 Real-Life Stories: Transcendence Through Desire

1. **The Accidental Mystic**

Case: Nia, a stressed-out grad student, discovered "microcosmic orbit" from an online video. She tried it one night when feeling random arousal but not wanting to release. Midway through, she experienced a rush of warmth and a sense of floating. Afterward, she felt calm, clear-headed, and oddly "at one with everything." She calls it her "mini Kundalini awakening."

2. Couple's Cosmic Union

Case: Bri and Devon, both curious about Tantra, decided to dedicate Sunday mornings to a slow, mindful intimacy session eye-gazing, breath syncing, and minimal movement. They report feeling "like one being" by the end, describing gentle waves of euphoria that left them giggly yet spiritually elevated for the rest of the day.

3. Solo Retreat Revelation

Case: Jordan, who identifies as "spiritual but not religious," went on a weekend cabin retreat alone. He practiced daily breathwork, sometimes stirring mild arousal intentionally, then meditating on it. On the final day, he felt a deep sense of **self-acceptance** and unconditional love for the world. He now incorporates a mini version of that routine every morning.

8.9 Practical Exercises: Deepening Spiritual Connection

Exercise 1: The Gratitude Flame

1. **Step 1**: Sit quietly, recall a memory that evokes gentle arousal.
2. **Step 2**: Visualize a flame in your heart center growing brighter with each breath.
3. **Step 3**: Mentally list 3 things you're grateful for, feeding that flame with each gratitude point.
4. **Step 4**: Conclude by bowing your head or placing a hand on your heart, honoring the energy you've cultivated.

Exercise 2: Orgasmic Prayer (Solo or Partnered)

1. **Step 1**: If you choose to release physically, do so mindfully slowing down, focusing on each sensation.
2. **Step 2**: At the peak of climax (or near it), mentally dedicate the energy to something greater love, compassion, healing for yourself or others.
3. **Step 3**: Post-release, spend a moment in stillness, letting that intention ripple through your consciousness.

Exercise 3: "Blue Ball" Meditation

1.   **Step 1**: If you're experiencing unfulfilled arousal (hello, comedic frustration), sit comfortably.
2.   **Step 2**: Inhale slowly, imagine that tension rising from your pelvic area up to your third eye (between the eyebrows).
3.   **Step 3**: Exhale, releasing any mental chatter, focusing on a sense of cosmic humor like, "Life is wild, and that's okay."
4.   **Step 4**: Repeat until the tension feels less urgent, replaced by a lighthearted calm.

8.10 Conclusion: From Earthly Desire to Cosmic Delight

Sexual transmutation can be a **bridge** between the mundane and the divine, turning everyday arousal into a stepping stone toward higher consciousness. Whether you resonate with kundalini, Tantra, or a more personal spiritual approach, the underlying principle remains: your body's desire can be a **sacred** force, guiding you toward unity, compassion, and an expanded sense of self.

Honor the Journey: There's no rush to "achieve enlightenment." Enjoy each moment, each spark of desire, each gentle wave of spiritual insight.

Stay Grounded: If you ever feel overwhelmed by intense experiences, anchor yourself with practical routines or professional support.

Celebrate the Mystery: Sexual energy is both playful and profound, comedic and cosmic. Embrace that paradox. It's part of the magic.

Next, we'll continue with **Part III**, exploring how to **prepare your mind**, develop the right **mindset**, and delve into **core techniques** for harnessing sexual energy in a daily, sustainable practice. Our *mindgasmic* voyage continues let's keep ascending!

CHAPTER 9

Preparing Your Mind: Mindset, Mindfulness, and Motivation

Up to now, we've covered how sexual transmutation can boost creativity, relationships, emotional well-being, and even spiritual growth. But there's one crucial element that underpins all these benefits: **your mindset**. If your mind is cluttered with doubts, distractions, or limiting beliefs, your ability to harness sexual energy diminishes.

In this chapter, we'll explore how to **prepare your mind** developing a resilient mindset, practicing mindfulness, and fueling your motivation so that when sexual energy arises (whether from a flirtatious encounter, a random fantasy, or "blue balls" frustration), you can channel it effectively.

9.1 Mindset Matters: From "I Can't" to "I'm Powered Up!"

1. Why Mindset is Everything

Think of your mind as the **operating system** for sexual transmutation. If it's bug-ridden with negativity or self-doubt, no amount of raw sexual energy will produce desired results.

Conversely, a growth-oriented mindset transforms that energy into rocket fuel for your goals.

2. Shifting from Shame to Celebration

Many people carry shame around sexuality maybe from upbringing, cultural norms, or past experiences. This shame can block your ability to see desire as positive.

The first step is **reframing**: sexual energy is a natural, vibrant resource, not a dirty secret. Remind yourself daily: "My desires fuel my life force."

3. Abundance vs. Scarcity

A scarcity mindset around pleasure or success can sabotage your transmutation efforts. If you believe there's "never enough" or "I'm unworthy," you'll resist harnessing sexual energy for fear of failing.

Adopt an abundance mindset: there's plenty of creative potential, emotional fulfillment, and yes, sexual energy, to go around.

Cheeky Note: Next time you catch yourself thinking, "Ugh, I shouldn't feel this arousal," pivot to, "Heck yes, my body is alive! Let's see how I can channel this juice." Instant reframe.

9.2 Mindfulness: The Glue that Binds Energy and Intention

1. Defining Mindfulness

Mindfulness is **paying attention** to the present moment with curiosity and non-judgment.

In sexual transmutation, mindfulness means noticing desire as it arises physically, emotionally, mentally and guiding it intentionally, rather than letting it hijack your day.

2. Everyday Mindfulness Practices

Breath Check: Pause every few hours, take three slow breaths, and ask, "What's my energy level right now?"

Body Scan: Before bed, mentally scan from toes to head, noticing tingles, tension, or warmth. This builds a map of your internal states crucial for identifying sexual energy.

3. Mindful Arousal

If you feel a sudden spark of lust, practice pausing. Label it: "I'm feeling turned on." No shame, no rush. Just recognition. Then decide: release it? Channel it? Store it for later?

This skill alone can revolutionize your approach, preventing impulsive decisions and encouraging strategic transmutation.

Comedic Perspective: Imagine you're a mad scientist in your own lab when that desire beaker starts bubbling, you calmly observe, "Ah, a reaction is occurring. Let's see how we can use this for the betterment of humankind (or at least my next project)!"

9.3 Motivation: Fanning the Flames of Desire-Driven Goals

1. Linking Sexual Energy to Your Aspirations

Sexual desire is inherently motivating like an internal cheerleader yelling, "Go get it!"

By associating that desire with a specific goal (finishing a novel, acing an exam, starting a business), you give your mind a reason to direct the energy there.

2. Goal-Setting Tips

Be Specific: "I want to channel my desire to write 500 words daily on my screenplay."

Tie Emotions: Imagine the thrill of success like the rush of a mild arousal and anchor that feeling to your goal. This emotional link keeps motivation high.

3. Mini-Milestones

Sexual transmutation works best in **sprints**. For instance, harness that wave of arousal for a 30-minute writing session. Reward yourself afterward with a short break or a comedic "blue balls" pun to keep it light.

Each mini-milestone achieved cements the habit: "When I feel desire, I create/achieve/do something meaningful."

9.4 Overcoming Internal Resistance: Doubt, Fear, and Distraction

1. Doubt

"Does this sexual transmutation stuff even work?"

Approach doubt as a curious skeptic. Try small experiments. When you see even minor results like writing a poem under mild arousal you'll build confidence in the process.

2. Fear of Success

Sometimes we fear the changes success might bring. If harnessing sexual energy makes you unstoppable, can you handle that level of responsibility or attention?

Reassure yourself: growth is natural, and you can adapt to new opportunities. Fear is just a sign you're pushing your limits.

3. Distraction Overload

Phones, social media, Netflix... oh my! If you're constantly bombarded by external stimuli, you won't notice or harness your internal energy.

Set "focus zones" where you silence notifications and tune into your body. This is where mindful arousal can flourish.

Cheeky Tip: If you're about to doom-scroll, but you notice a flutter of desire, pivot: "Wait, let me see if I can channel this flutter into finishing that chore I've been avoiding." The comedic irony can be your ally "I used sexual tension to do the laundry; who knew adulting could be this fun?"

9.5 Affirmations and Mental Conditioning

1. Affirmations 101

Short, powerful statements that reinforce a positive belief. E.g., "My sexual energy fuels my creativity."

Repeat them when you sense desire, effectively linking the state of arousal to constructive self-talk.

2. Visualization

Envision yourself confidently directing sexual energy into a task maybe you see a swirl of red or orange light moving from your lower abdomen to your head, powering your ideas.

The brain responds to imagined scenarios similarly to real ones, strengthening neural pathways.

3. Journaling

Keep a daily log of moments you felt desire and how you used (or didn't use) it. Over time, patterns emerge, helping you refine your approach.

Celebrate small wins: "Today, I felt a midday spark and wrote two pages of my short story!"

9.6 Cultivating a Daily Practice: Consistency is King (or Queen)

1. Morning Check-In

Spend 5 minutes upon waking to breathe, sense your body, and set an intention for your sexual energy that day.

Example: "Any desire I feel today, I'll channel into completing my tasks at work with flair."

2. Midday Mindfulness

A quick 1-minute "body scan" before lunch or after a flirty text. Notice if you can sense a flicker of arousal. If yes, decide how to use it maybe you'll tackle a tough email or design a creative pitch.

3. Evening Reflection

Journal or mentally review: Did you harness any sexual sparks? Did you slip into autopilot? No judgment just learning.

This consistent routine cements the habit, making transmutation second nature.

9.7 Real-Life Anecdotes: Mindset Triumphs

1. Bella's Story

Challenge: Bella felt ashamed of her high libido, often labeling herself "too sexual."

Shift: She started repeating, "My desire is my power," each time she felt a tingle. Within weeks, she noticed more confidence at work, volunteering for leadership roles without hesitation.

2. Ray's Revelation

Challenge: Ray was easily distracted he'd get lost in social media whenever he felt bored or a mild attraction to someone online.

Shift: He implemented a midday breath check, noticing that boredom was sometimes mild arousal in disguise. Channeling it into coding projects, he ended up launching a profitable app side hustle.

3. Tammy's Turnaround

Challenge: Tammy doubted sexual transmutation was real. She decided to run a "fun experiment" for a week documenting every time she felt desire and trying to channel it into her new fitness routine.

Result: By day 5, she was hitting personal records in her workouts, fueled by micro-surges of arousal. She's now a believer.

9.8 Practical Exercises: Mindset, Mindfulness, and Motivation

Exercise 1: The Desire Journal

1.   **Step 1**: Each morning, note your baseline mood.
2.   **Step 2**: Throughout the day, record moments of sexual desire or mild arousal (time, trigger, intensity).
3.   **Step 3**: Write how you responded did you redirect it, ignore it, or seek physical release?
4.   **Step 4**: Summarize each evening. Notice patterns or repeated triggers. Over a week, you'll see where mindset shifts are needed.

Exercise 2: Breath-Anchor Affirmations

1.   **Step 1**: Sit comfortably, close your eyes.
2.   **Step 2**: Inhale slowly, mentally saying, "I welcome my sexual energy."

3. **Step 3**: Exhale slowly, mentally saying, "I direct it toward my highest goals."
4. **Step 4**: Repeat for 2–3 minutes, noticing any tingles or warmth. Let that sensation reinforce the affirmation.

Exercise 3: The "Flirty Task" Challenge

1. **Step 1**: Identify a task you've been procrastinating on.
2. **Step 2**: Conjure a mild flirty or sensual memory, letting your body feel a small surge.
3. **Step 3**: Immediately tackle the task for at least 10 minutes.
4. **Step 4**: Celebrate any progress with a playful note in your journal or a quick comedic "blue ball" pun to keep it fun.

9.9 Conclusion: A Mind Primed for Power

1.2 Partnered Exercises

A **growth-oriented, mindful**, and **motivated** mind is the perfect soil for planting the seeds of sexual transmutation. Without this mental groundwork, your desire might fizzle out or lead to impulsive choices. But with it, you become a conductor, skillfully orchestrating the symphony of your sexual energy into productivity, creativity, emotional well-being, and beyond.

Stay Curious: Mindset work is ongoing. Keep refining your beliefs, and don't shy away from comedic self-awareness.

Practice Mindfulness: Let every wave of arousal be an opportunity to deepen presence and intention.

Fuel Your Goals: Attach your sexual spark to real-life aspirations, watching them flourish under this unique brand of energy.

Next, we'll dive into the **core techniques** for harnessing sexual energy building on the mental foundation you've just set. Ready to roll up your sleeves (or maybe roll them down for some breathwork)? Let's go!

CHAPTER 10

Core Techniques for Harnessing Sexual Energy: Your Roadmap to Daily Practice

You've laid the mental groundwork, embraced mindfulness, and stoked your motivation. Now it's time to get **hands-on** figuratively (and sometimes literally). This chapter provides a **roadmap** of core techniques that anchor sexual transmutation in **daily practice**. Think of these as your go-to methods whenever you feel that spark, want to build a reservoir of energy, or simply need a comedic break from the "blue ball" tension.

10.1 The Spectrum of Techniques

1. Subtle to Intense

Techniques vary from gentle breathwork and visualization to more advanced, physically engaging methods. Start where you're comfortable.

Not everyone wants to practice edging or advanced retention. That's okay. Pick and choose what resonates.

2. Solo vs. Partnered

Many techniques can be done alone or adapted for a partner. We'll note where synergy might enhance the experience (though we have dedicated partnered chapters coming up).

Even if you're in a relationship, solo practice can deepen your self-awareness, making partnered experiences richer.

3. Consistency is Key

Like learning an instrument, these techniques yield the best results when practiced regularly. Sporadic attempts might still help, but routine fosters mastery.

Cheeky Perspective: Think of these as sexual transmutation "recipes." Some are appetizers (quick breath fixes), others are full-course feasts (edging, advanced orbits). Try them out and see what flavors suit your palate.

10.2 Breathwork and Visualization: The Foundation

Technique 1: Microcosmic Orbit (Taoist Classic)

1. **Sit Comfortably:** Spine upright, shoulders relaxed.
2. **Inhale:** Imagine energy rising up your spine from the tailbone to the crown of your head.
3. **Exhale:** Guide the energy down the front of your body, returning it to the lower abdomen (the "dantian").
4. **Include Mild Arousal:** If you sense a spark, let that warmth ride along the orbit. Over time, you'll feel a continuous loop of energy.

Why It Works: This technique is a **tried-and-true** Taoist method for circulating chi (life force). Adding sexual energy supercharges it, preventing "stagnation" in the lower regions perfect if you're dealing with comedic "blue ball" tension or want a gentle daily practice.

Technique 2: The Flame Path

1. **Visualize a Flame:** Close your eyes, see a small flame in your pelvis or lower abdomen.
2. **Grow the Flame:** With each inhale, let it grow brighter. With each exhale, let it rise slightly upward chest, throat, or head.
3. **Savor the Warmth:** If arousal spikes, don't shy away. Let the flame incorporate that heat, fueling a sense of inner radiance.
4. **Completion:** End by mentally placing the flame in your heart, feeling gratitude for your body's energy.

Why It Works: This is a more **imaginative** approach, great for those who love visualization. It can transform raw desire into a cozy, uplifting sensation that lights up your day (pun intended).

10.3 Retention and Edging: Harnessing the "Almost There" Tension

1. Defining Edging

Edging means bringing yourself (solo or partnered) close to orgasm, then pausing before crossing the finish line. This pause accumulates **intense** energy in your body.

If repeated, you build a reservoir of desire that can be directed into creativity, workouts, or any goal needing a boost.

2. Practical Steps

• **Awareness**: Notice the "point of no return" and stop just before. Breathe. Let the tension swirl.

Mindful Pause: Visualize that tension moving up your spine or into your heart.

Repeat: You can do multiple rounds if comfortable, or just once. The key is to maintain a safe, enjoyable level of arousal without forcing yourself into discomfort.

3. Pros and Cons

Pros: Rapid surge of energy, heightened sensitivity, and a sense of playful control over your body.

Cons: Overdo it, and you might end up with serious frustration (our old friend "blue balls"). Know your limits.

Comedic Perspective: Think of edging like cooking pasta. You want it al dente firm but not fully done. Overcook it, and you lose the tension. Undercook it, and you might be unsatisfied. Find that sweet spot!

10.4 Solo Sensual Practices: Nurturing the Self

1. Self-Massage for Energy Flow

Use oils or lotions. Gently explore your body, focusing on non-genital areas first.

Breathe deeply, imagining each stroke guiding energy from your extremities toward your core.

If arousal emerges, welcome it. Pause occasionally to let the sensation spread upward.

2. Sensual Movement or Dance

Put on music that evokes a mild sensuality. Move your hips, sway, let your arms flow.

The goal isn't to look sexy for anyone else; it's to feel the **rhythm** of your body. This can unlock stuck energy, turning a random "I'm kinda turned on" moment into a mini dance party.

3. Mindful Pleasure Sessions

If you choose to engage in self-pleasure, do it with **intention**. Slow down. Focus on each sensation. If you near orgasm, consider pausing (edging) or directing the energy to your heart or third eye via visualization.

This approach transforms a routine act into a meditative, transmutative experience.

10.5 Partnered Exploration (Overview)

(We'll have dedicated chapters on partnered exercises, but here's a sneak peek of core techniques.)

1. Teasing and Pausing

Similar to edging, but with a partner. You both bring each other close, then pause to breathe, gaze into each other's eyes, and channel that combined tension into shared intentions.

2. Energy Sharing

One partner places a hand over the other's lower abdomen while the receiving partner focuses on drawing energy upward. You alternate roles, synchronizing breath.

This fosters trust and a sense of "we're in this together."

3. Yab Yum Pose

A classic Tantric position where one partner sits cross-legged, and the other sits on their lap, also cross-legged, facing them. Heart centers align, and you can breathe in sync. Sexual energy becomes a **shared** circuit.

Why It Works: Partnered techniques amplify sexual energy exponentially. You're no longer dealing with your own spark but a **collective flame**. That said, it requires open communication, trust, and mutual comfort with occasional comedic tension ("Wait, we're both turned on are we sure we're not finishing yet?").

10.6 Quick-Fix Techniques for Busy Lives

1. 30-Second Arousal Redirect

If you feel a sudden surge (like a text from a crush) but have a busy schedule, do a **quick breath**: Inhale the excitement, exhale directing it to your head or heart. Then immediately tackle a small task.

This micro-practice can keep you from spiraling into a 20-minute fantasy or phone-scrolling session.

2. "Spark & Sprint"

Next time you sense mild arousal and need to do a short burst of work, harness it. Set a timer for 10 minutes, ride that wave of focus, then break.

Even short bursts, repeated throughout the day, can significantly boost productivity.

3. Comedic Self-Talk

If tension builds and you can't address it physically, adopt a playful mantra: "I'm storing this sexy charge for my afternoon meeting watch me shine!" Laugh at the absurdity, and you'll find the tension more manageable.

10.7 Real-Life Anecdotes: Core Techniques in Action

1. Marisol's Microcosmic Win

Scenario: She learned the Microcosmic Orbit from an online tutorial. During a random midday flush of desire, she practiced it for 2 minutes in the office restroom.

Outcome: Felt invigorated, knocked out her project proposal in record time. She jokes that the restroom became her "secret chamber of power."

2. Jonah's Edging Experiment

Scenario: Jonah tried edging while writing music. He'd get close to climax, pause, and record guitar riffs while the tension was high.

Outcome: He produced some of his most energetic tracks, describing the process as "weirdly fun and creatively explosive."

3. Tina & Greg's Quick-Fix Spark

Scenario: A busy couple with kids, they barely had time for full intimacy. They discovered the "30-Second Arousal Redirect."

Outcome: Whenever a quick flirty moment arose, they'd breathe, exchange a knowing look, and then each tackle chores or work tasks with renewed pep. They said it "kept the romance alive in the chaos of parenting."

10.8 Practical Exercises: Your Daily Roadmap

Exercise 1: Morning Orbit Routine

1. **Step 1**: Upon waking, sit on your bed or a cushion.
2. **Step 2**: Perform 5–10 cycles of the Microcosmic Orbit, gently guiding any mild arousal upward.
3. **Step 3**: Set an intention like "Today, I channel this energy into my meetings with calm confidence."

Exercise 2: Midday Flame

1. **Step 1**: At lunch or a work break, close your eyes for 2 minutes.
2. **Step 2**: Visualize a small flame in your lower abdomen. If you sense any sexual warmth, feed it to the flame.

3.   **Step 3**: Exhale, letting the flame rise to your heart or mind. Return to work with that glow.

Exercise 3: Evening Edging (Optional)

1.   **Step 1**: If comfortable, engage in self-pleasure.
2.   **Step 2**: Edge at least once pause near orgasm, breathe deeply, let the tension swirl.
3.   **Step 3**: If you decide to release, do so mindfully, imagining the orgasmic energy spreading through your entire body. If you choose not to release, channel the tension into journaling or creative tasks.

10.9 Conclusion: Building Your Personal Toolkit

The core techniques in this chapter offer a **menu** of ways to harness sexual energy. Whether you prefer gentle breathwork, playful edging, or quick-fix "spark & sprint" methods, the key is to **experiment** and find what resonates with your lifestyle and comfort level.

Be Consistent: Like any skill, mastery comes with regular practice.

Stay Lighthearted: Sexual tension can be comedic. Embrace the humor let it fuel your creativity, not stifle it.

Refine & Adapt: As you grow, you might discover advanced practices or combine techniques. Keep evolving your personal approach.

Next up, we'll expand on **guided meditations, breathwork** specifics, and **solo practices** in Chapter 11, giving you even more detail to fine-tune your *mindgasmic* journey. Let's keep the momentum rolling there's so much more to explore!

CHAPTER 11

Guided Meditations, Breathwork, and Solo Practices: Deepening Your Personal Exploration

We've laid out core techniques for harnessing sexual energy now let's go **deeper**. In this chapter, we'll explore **guided meditations, specialized breathwork**, and **solo practices** that can help you refine your transmutation skills. Whether you're new to meditation or an experienced yogi, these practices can open fresh avenues for creativity, emotional balance, and that trademark *mindgasmic* spark.

11.1 Why Guided Meditations and Breathwork?

1. Structured Focus

Sometimes, it's challenging to sit down and just "feel" sexual energy without distraction. Guided meditations offer a **step-by-step** roadmap to keep you on track.

Breathwork helps you anchor wandering thoughts, channeling your arousal where you want it (heart, mind, or creative impulses).

2. Gentle Entry Point

If you're apprehensive about edging or advanced retention, meditations and breath exercises provide a **gentle introduction** to transmutation.

You can dip your toes in the water, exploring mild arousal states without pushing yourself too far.

3. Consistency & Growth

Meditative practices become more powerful with repetition. Over time, you'll notice heightened self-awareness, deeper emotional intelligence, and a more playful attitude toward desire.

Cheeky Note: Think of guided meditations as the "GPS" for your sexual energy. Instead of aimlessly wandering, you have a friendly voice (possibly your own or a recorded track) saying, "Turn left at the sacral chakra. Proceed straight toward your heart center. Destination: mind-blowing clarity."

11.2 Setting the Stage: Environment & Mindset

1. Create a Sacred Space

Dim the lights, light a candle, or play soft instrumental music. Even if you're just in a corner of your bedroom, add a little flair a cozy pillow, a favorite scent.

This cues your mind: "Time to relax, explore, and transmute."

2. Choose Comfort Over Formality

You don't have to contort into a lotus pose if that's uncomfortable. Sit or lie in a posture that allows you to breathe deeply and maintain some alertness.

If you prefer wearing comfy pyjamas or nothing at all go for it. This is **your** practice.

3. Embrace a Lighthearted Attitude

If you giggle at the start maybe feeling silly about meditating on your sexual energy that's okay. Laughter can release tension, ironically making you **more** receptive to deeper experiences.

11.3 Guided Meditation Scripts: Step-by-Step

Below are three in-depth scripts you can record on your phone, read aloud, or memorize. Adjust the pacing to suit your comfort level.

Meditation 1: The Heart-Warmth Journey

Purpose: Transform mild arousal into a soothing wave of compassion and self-love.

1. Settle In (2 minutes)

Sit or lie down, close your eyes. Take a few slow, steady breaths. Feel the surface beneath you soft, supportive.

If you sense any tension in your body, gently release it on each exhale.

2. Arousal Awareness (2 minutes)

Gently recall a moment that sparks mild desire maybe a flirty smile or a sweet touch. Let the memory warm you, but keep it around a 3–4 on the arousal scale.

Notice any sensations in your lower abdomen, chest, or limbs.

3. Guiding the Warmth (3 minutes)

Imagine the warmth in your lower abdomen glowing like a small sun. With each inhale, visualize that glow expanding.

As you exhale, let it drift upward into your chest, like a gentle breeze carrying a warm mist.

4. Heart Embrace (3 minutes)

Envision this glow settling in your heart center. Each breath fans the glow, intensifying feelings of compassion and self-love.

Mentally affirm: "I direct my desire toward love and kindness for myself and others."

5. Integration (2 minutes)

Rest in the sensation of a warm, open heart. If thoughts arise, acknowledge them and return to your breath.

Conclude by taking a deep inhale, exhale slowly, and open your eyes when ready.

(Total ~12 minutes. Extend or shorten as needed.)

Meditation 2: The Microcosmic Orbit Extended

Purpose: Circulate sexual energy through the classic Taoist loop, integrating it into a calm, balanced state.

1. Centering (2 minutes)

Sit upright. Relax your shoulders. Place your hands on your lower abdomen. Inhale, feeling your belly expand; exhale, feeling it contract.

If you sense a flicker of arousal, acknowledge it kindly, letting it build gently.

2. Energy Path Awareness (3 minutes)

Inhale: Imagine energy rising from the base of your spine (tailbone) up your back to the crown of your head.

Exhale: Guide it down the front of your body, returning to your lower abdomen. Visualize a smooth circuit.

3. Incorporate Arousal (3 minutes)

Let any sexual warmth join this orbit. Each inhale pulls the warmth upward; each exhale recirculates it down.

If you feel an urge to intensify arousal, do so mindfully maybe recalling a gentle fantasy or memory.

4. Pause & Hold (2 minutes)

Occasionally, pause the orbit at your crown or heart center for one breath cycle, letting the warmth gather. Then continue the flow.

This "hold" amplifies energy in that spot.

5. Closing (2 minutes)

Visualize the orbit gradually slowing. Let the energy rest in your lower abdomen, like a battery storing power.

End with a final deep breath, open your eyes softly, and note any sensations or clarity.

(Total ~12 minutes. Adjust timing as desired.)

Meditation 3: The Inner Flame of Creation

Purpose: Ignite creative inspiration by merging mild arousal with a visualization of your creative or professional goals.

1. Relax & Breathe (2 minutes)

Sit or lie comfortably. Take several slow breaths, releasing daily stress.

Allow your mind to drift to a calm, receptive state.

2. Spark the Flame (2 minutes)

Recall a memory or fantasy that sparks mild arousal just enough to feel a gentle warmth in your lower abdomen.

Picture that warmth as a small flame.

3. Fuel the Flame with Goals (3 minutes)

Now, bring to mind a creative or professional goal a project you're passionate about or a skill you want to improve.

Each inhale "feeds" the flame with your desire; each exhale directs that combined energy toward your goal. See the flame grow, fueled by your ambition and arousal.

4. Sense the Expansion (3 minutes)

Let the flame expand in your torso, radiating up to your head. Imagine sparks of inspiration swirling in your mind.

Mentally affirm: "My desire fuels my creativity. I am energized and inspired."

5. Completion & Grounding (2 minutes)

Slowly let the flame settle in your lower abdomen, like an ember that stays warm, ready for use.

Open your eyes, journal any immediate ideas or solutions that arise.

(Total ~12 minutes. Tweak timings as you see fit.)

11.4 Specialized Breathwork for Sexual Transmutation

1. Box Breathing with Arousal Focus

Inhale 4 counts, hold 4 counts, exhale 4 counts, hold 4 counts.

During the hold phases, gently recall a sensual memory or let your body sense mild tension.

This rhythmic approach can calm your mind while amplifying sexual awareness.

2. Alternate Nostril Breathing

Traditionally a yogic practice for balancing left/right brain hemispheres.

If you're feeling sexual tension in one part of your body, imagine each inhale drawing energy from that area up to your head, each exhale releasing mental clutter.

A quick fix for midday stress or if you feel "on edge" (in both the sexual and emotional sense).

3. Fire Breath (Kapalabhati)

Rapid, forceful exhales through the nose, with passive inhales.

Not recommended if you're new to breathwork start slowly. But once comfortable, this can ignite a **vibrant** surge of energy.

If sexual desire surfaces, let it ride the waves of your exhales, fueling a sense of internal "fire."

Caution: If you feel dizzy or overwhelmed, pause. Some breathwork is intense. Always honor your body's signals.

11.5 Solo Practices Beyond Meditation: Expanding Your Self-Exploration

1. Mindful Self-Touch (Non-Orgasmic)

Gently explore your body with oil or lotion, focusing on sensations rather than reaching climax.

This fosters a deeper relationship with your physical self, helping you identify subtle cues of arousal.

Great for releasing tension while preserving energy for transmutation.

2. Sensual Baths

Light candles, add essential oils or bath salts, and soak. Let the warm water and mild arousal combine into a meditative experience.

If you feel that *tingle*, direct it toward releasing stress from your muscles or envisioning creative solutions.

3. Chakra Visualization in the Mirror

Stand or sit before a mirror, minimal clothing or naked if comfortable.

Scan each chakra region root to crown imagining sexual energy rising. Affirm your body's beauty and your energy's power.

Combines body positivity with spiritual transmutation.

Cheeky Tip: If you catch yourself thinking, "This is so silly I'm naked in front of a mirror, imagining swirling lights," just grin. A little comedic acceptance can break self-consciousness, opening the door to genuine transformation.

11.6 Addressing Potential Pitfalls: Over-Stimulation, Guilt, and "Blue Ball" Frustration

1. Over-Stimulation

If you find these practices intensify arousal too much, making you anxious or antsy, step back. Try shorter sessions or gentler fantasies.

Balance is key sexual energy should **empower**, not overwhelm.

2. Guilt or Shame

Old beliefs might resurface: "Am I being indulgent?" or "This is weird." Gently remind yourself: you're nurturing your own vitality.

A supportive therapist or trusted friend can help dismantle deep-seated shame if it persists.

3. "Blue Ball" Woes

If tension accumulates uncomfortably, consider partial release or a comedic acceptance: "Alright, body, you're raring to go. Let's redirect this into a creative sprint!"

Alternatively, a quick orgasmic release can be a valid choice. Transmutation is about **options**, not forced retention.

11.7 Real-Life Anecdotes: Transformations Through Guided Practices

1. Lucia's Creative Renaissance

Scenario: A children's book illustrator, Lucia felt blocked. She started a nightly 10-minute "Flame Path" meditation, lightly stirring arousal.

Result: Within weeks, she was sketching new characters with renewed passion. She credits the flame visualization for unlocking her playful spirit.

2. Omar's Confidence Boost

Scenario: Omar struggled with self-doubt, especially in social settings. He tried the Heart-Warmth Journey each morning, merging mild arousal with compassion for himself.

Result: Over a month, friends noticed he seemed calmer, more open. Omar says, "It's like I harnessed my nerves and turned them into a gentle power source."

3. Serena's Stress Relief

Scenario: A grad student with high anxiety, Serena discovered Box Breathing with a pinch of sensual recall. She'd do it before Zoom presentations.

Result: Her anxiety reduced, and she delivered her research findings with clarity. She calls it her "secret superpower."

11.8 Practical Exercises: Integrating Guided Meditations & Breathwork

Exercise 1: The 7-Day Meditation Challenge

1. **Step 1**: Choose one of the three guided meditations above (Heart-Warmth, Microcosmic Orbit, or Inner Flame).
2. **Step 2**: Commit to practicing it daily for 7 days, at roughly the same time.
3. **Step 3**: Journal any changes in mood, creativity, or stress levels.
4. **Step 4**: If you skip a day, no guilt just resume the next day.

Exercise 2: Midday Breath Check (5-Minute Practice)

1. **Step 1**: Set a phone alarm for midday (or whenever you hit a slump).
2. **Step 2**: Perform a chosen breath technique (Box, Alternate Nostril, or Fire Breath) for 2–3 minutes.
3. **Step 3**: Notice if any arousal surfaces. If yes, gently swirl it upward on your exhales.
4. **Step 4**: Return to your task, harnessing the renewed focus.

Exercise 3: Solo Sensual Ritual

1. **Step 1**: Allocate 15–20 minutes in a calm environment maybe after a bath or shower.
2. **Step 2**: Combine gentle self-touch with slow, mindful breathing. No orgasmic goal; just sensation and exploration.
3. **Step 3**: If arousal builds, try directing it up your spine. Pause often, savoring each wave.
4. **Step 4**: Conclude by thanking your body for its vitality, then ground yourself with a drink of water or journaling.

11.9 Conclusion: Your Personal Playground of Practice

Guided meditations, specialized breathwork, and solo exploration form a **powerful trifecta** for sexual transmutation. By weaving these practices into your daily routine, you'll gain a richer, more nuanced relationship with your body, your emotions, and your creativity.

Experiment Freely: Not every script or breath technique will click. That's okay tweak them, combine them, or craft your own.

Stay Playful: Humor dissolves tension, keeps you from taking it all too seriously, and ironically allows deeper experiences to unfold.

Build Consistency: A few minutes daily can yield exponential benefits over time.

Next, we'll move to **Chapter 12**, focusing on **partnered exercises** and deeper intimacy because while solo practice is transformative, sharing sexual transmutation with a partner can unlock a whole new dimension of connection. Let's continue this *mindgasmic* adventure!

CHAPTER 12

Partnered Exercises and Deeper Intimacy: Harnessing Desire as a Dynamic Duo

We've explored how to cultivate sexual energy on your own now let's shift gears to **partnered** experiences. When two people unite their energies, the results can be **exponential**. Think of it like combining two power grids: you don't just double the electricity; you create a **synergistic** effect that can elevate both partners physically, emotionally, and even spiritually.

This chapter focuses on **practical** partnered exercises to deepen intimacy, enhance communication, and transform everyday desire into a shared journey of discovery.

12.1 Why Partnered Transmutation?

1. Shared Goals, Shared Growth

Sexual transmutation in a relationship isn't just about better sex it's about aligning energies for **mutual aspirations**.

Couples who practice can direct their combined spark toward building a dream home, launching a business, or nurturing a family.

2. Amplified Emotional Connection

Harnessing sexual desire as a team fosters **vulnerability**, **trust**, and **empathy**. You're not just satisfying a physical urge; you're forging a bond that transcends routine intimacy.

3. Conflict Resolution

As we touched on earlier, the same tension that can lead to bickering can also be harnessed to unify. Partnered transmutation helps reframe friction into fuel for collaboration.

Comedic Angle: Next time you're both in a mood but decide to hold off on release, you might say, "We're saving this for tomorrow's big pitch at work." Laugh together, feeling like secret agents of desire, re-channeling tension into success.

12.2 Foundational Elements: Communication, Consent, and Comfort

1. Communication is Key

Before diving into partnered transmutation, have an open talk. Share your curiosity, potential awkwardness, and hopes.

Encourage your partner to express their comfort level. If they're hesitant, suggest starting with simpler, less intense exercises.

2. Consent and Boundaries

Sexual transmutation is never about **coercing** your partner to do something they're uncomfortable with.

Both parties should feel safe pausing or shifting gears at any point. A simple phrase like "Let's take a breath break" can help.

3. Comfort is Priority

Ensure you both feel physically comfortable room temperature, lighting, clothing (or lack thereof).

If either of you experiences pain, emotional distress, or comedic "this is too weird" vibes, it's okay to stop or pivot.

12.3 Partnered Exercises: Step-by-Step Guides

Exercise 1: Synced Breathing & Eye Gazing

Purpose: Build emotional and energetic harmony.

1. Setup

Sit facing each other, legs crossed if comfortable. Keep a slight distance so you can maintain soft eye contact.

Rest your hands on your own knees or hold hands gently.

2. **Breath Sync (2–3 minutes)**

Close your eyes. One partner begins a slow inhale; the other tries to match that inhale. Then exhale together.

Feel the rise and fall of your chests in unison. This might cause giggles embrace it as part of the bonding.

3. **Open Eyes, Maintain Rhythm (2–3 minutes)**

Now open your eyes, continue breathing together. Look into each other's eyes softly, not staring forcefully but staying present.

If you sense a flicker of sexual tension, let it be. Smile if it feels natural.

4. **Optional Intention (1–2 minutes)**

After a few minutes, one partner can whisper an intention, like "We channel our shared energy into deeper understanding."

The other partner can echo or offer a complementary intention.

5. **Closing**

Gently break eye contact, share a hug or a light kiss. Notice the calm unity you've established.

(Total ~10 minutes. Adjust as you like.)

Comedic Tip: If one of you bursts out laughing mid-exercise, roll with it. Laughter can release tension and ironically deepen the intimacy.

Exercise 2: The Tease & Pause (Partnered Edging)

Purpose: Build intense sexual tension together, then redirect it into emotional or creative synergy.

1. **Set the Mood**

Dim lights, play soft music. Decide on a safe word or phrase if either partner feels overwhelmed ("Let's pivot" or "Time out").

Agree on the level of clothing removal, if any.

2. Initial Arousal (5–10 minutes)

Engage in gentle touching, kissing, or cuddling that arouses both of you. Aim for a moderate level of excitement maybe a 5 or 6 on the 1–10 scale.

3. Pause & Breathe (2–3 minutes)

When you feel you could escalate further, pause all movement. Breathe deeply in sync, letting the tension remain.

Mentally or verbally say: "We hold this energy for something greater."

4. Communication Check (1 minute)

Whisper or speak softly: "How are you feeling?" "Is this comfortable?" "Shall we keep going?"

If yes, resume gentle arousal. If not, channel the tension into a cuddle or conversation.

5. Repeat Cycles

You can do multiple tease-and-pause rounds, each time intensifying desire. The key is not to rush to orgasm.

After 2–3 cycles, you'll have a significant reservoir of tension to direct.

6. Optional Redirection

Channel the energy into a shared goal. For instance, talk about a project or dream you both have. Feel the spark fueling your conversation.

If you choose to end with orgasm, do so mindfully, perhaps dedicating that release to mutual well-being.

(Total time can vary from 15 minutes to an hour, depending on your comfort and schedule.)

Comedic Tip: If one partner jokes, "I can't take it anymore I have the worst case of blue balls," you can either choose to transform it into laughter therapy or shift to a partial release. The key is mutual respect and fun.

Exercise 3: Sensual Massage with Intent

Purpose: Nurture intimacy, relaxation, and subtle arousal without rushing to release.

1. Set Up the Space

Use a comfortable bed or floor mat, have massage oil ready, and keep towels handy.

Soft, soothing music helps maintain a relaxed atmosphere.

2. Decide on Roles

One partner gives the massage first, while the other receives. You can switch later.

The giver's mindset: "I channel my sexual energy into these nurturing touches."

3. Slow, Mindful Touch (10–15 minutes)

Begin with the receiver's back, using gentle strokes. Breathe in sync if possible.

Let the giver focus on each muscle group, occasionally pausing to sense if the receiver's arousal is building.

4. Arousal Check

If the receiver feels a surge of desire, they can communicate: "I'm feeling a wave let's pause and breathe."

The giver can rest their hands softly, both inhaling that energy, exhaling it into the air or "sending" it to a shared intention.

5. Switch or Conclude

After 10–15 minutes, switch roles if you like. Or conclude with a cuddling session, letting the shared warmth linger.

This practice fosters deep trust and can be done weekly or whenever you both crave a slow, intimate connection.

Cheeky Note: Sensual massage can be comedic if someone's ticklish or if oil spills. Laugh it off. A bit of clumsiness can heighten the sense of genuine, playful intimacy.

12.4 Emotional Depth and Communication Exercises

1. "We Desire" Journaling

After a tease-and-pause session or sensual massage, grab a journal. Each partner writes a short paragraph about what they desire personally, professionally, or as a couple.

Then share aloud. This is a powerful way to harness the post-arousal clarity for honest communication.

2. Heart-to-Heart Confessions

During mild arousal (say a gentle cuddle), each partner confesses something they appreciate about the other, or a small worry that's been on their mind.

Sexual tension can embolden vulnerability, turning "I'm nervous about my job" into a heartfelt moment of support.

3. Conflict Transmutation

If you sense conflict brewing, try a quick breath sync before diving into the discussion. Acknowledge any underlying sexual frustration or emotional tension.

Use that tension as a **shared** challenge like, "We have this big ball of energy between us; let's direct it to solve our disagreement, not fuel it."

12.5 Common Pitfalls in Partnered Transmutation

1. Misaligned Desires

One partner might be all-in, the other lukewarm. Respect boundaries and find a middle ground perhaps simpler exercises or shorter sessions.

2. Performance Pressure

Avoid turning these exercises into a "must achieve mindgasmic synergy" chore. It's about exploration, not ticking boxes.

If frustration arises, pivot to a comedic perspective: "Hey, we tried something new, it was awkward, but at least we laughed."

3. Overemphasis on Sexual Acts

Remember, sexual transmutation includes but isn't limited to sexual activity. If you or your partner is uninterested in physical intimacy at times, you can still channel mild desire or emotional closeness into other shared goals.

Cheeky Tip: If either partner jokes, "This is feeling like homework," take a break. Grab snacks, watch a silly show, and come back when you're in a lighter mood.

12.6 Real-Life Anecdotes: Couples and the Power of Partnered Practice

1. Erin & Marcus: The Startup Success

Scenario: They launched a small tech startup together. Stress soared, intimacy plummeted. They tried weekly "Tease & Pause" sessions, redirecting that tension into brainstorming.

Outcome: They report "creative fireworks" in their pitch meetings the day after a session, attributing the synergy to harnessed sexual energy.

2. Dani & Jo: Healing Past Trauma

Scenario: Both had relationship baggage. They used gentle "Synced Breathing & Eye Gazing" to rebuild trust.

Outcome: Over months, they developed a deeper emotional bond, finding that shared breath and mild arousal dissolved old fears. "It felt like we re-taught each other what safety in intimacy means," Jo said.

3. Sophie & Li: Rekindling the Spark

Scenario: Married for 12 years, sexual routine felt stale. They added sensual massage nights, focusing on slow, mindful touch without rushing to orgasm.

Outcome: They rediscovered each other's bodies with a fresh perspective, reporting "honeymoon vibes" after each session.

12.7 Practical Exercises: Strengthening Partnered Transmutation

Exercise 1: "We Breathe as One" (10-Minute Daily Practice)

1. **Step 1**: Each evening, sit facing each other for 2 minutes of synced breathing.
2. **Step 2**: Exchange a brief affirmation "I see you, I appreciate you."
3. **Step 3**: If a mild spark arises, hold hands, breathe for 2 more minutes, letting that spark fuel gratitude.
4. **Step 4**: End with a hug or a gentle kiss. Keep it short, consistent, and loving.

Exercise 2: Partnered "Flame Path" (15–20 minutes)

1. **Step 1**: Each partner visualizes a small flame in their lower abdomen.
2. **Step 2**: Hold hands, imagining your flames merging through your palms.
3. **Step 3**: If you sense arousal, let the flame brighten. Breathe slowly, sending the combined flame up your spines.
4. **Step 4**: After a few minutes, verbally share one goal or dream. Let the flame represent your shared energy fueling that dream.

Exercise 3: Post-Intimacy Journaling

1. **Step 1**: After any intimate session (be it teasing, massage, or orgasmic release), take 5 minutes to jot down how you feel.
2. **Step 2**: Each partner can note any insights, ideas, or emotions that surfaced.
3. **Step 3**: Share highlights, reinforcing that sexual energy isn't just physical it's a wellspring of personal and relational insight.

12.8 Conclusion: Building a Dynamic Duo

Partnered sexual transmutation transforms your relationship into a **collaborative adventure**, where both of you harness desire to fuel creativity, emotional depth, and shared ambitions. Whether you're gently flirting, practicing advanced edging, or just breathing together, the synergy you create can ripple through every aspect of your life.

Stay Open: Not every exercise will feel natural at first. Embrace trial, error, and comedic mishaps.

Celebrate Each Win: If a session brings you closer, or you both handle stress better the next day, acknowledge that success.

Grow Together: As you evolve individually, your partnership evolves too. Keep communication flowing, adapting exercises to your changing needs.

With this foundation of **partnered intimacy**, we'll move on to **Chapter 13**, where we'll discuss **applying sexual transmutation in daily life** from mundane chores to major life decisions. Because yes, even your grocery shopping can become a *mindgasmic* experience if you channel desire the right way. Let's keep going!

CHAPTER 13

Applying Sexual Transmutation in Daily Life: From Mundane to Mind-Blowing

We've covered the foundations, techniques, and partnered dynamics of sexual transmutation. But how do you actually weave it into your **everyday routine** the grocery runs, work meetings, random errands, or even your morning commute? This chapter is all about bridging the gap between theory and practice, transforming your **mundane moments** into *mindgasmic* opportunities for growth, creativity, and fun.

13.1 The Power of Small Moments

1. Why Small Moments Matter

Life isn't just epic projects and steamy bedroom sessions. It's also waiting in line at the bank, folding laundry, and answering emails.

These "in-between" moments can become micro-chances for sexual transmutation quick mental pivots that harness mild arousal or tension into productivity or emotional uplift.

2. Making It Second Nature

When you consistently apply transmutation in small bursts, it becomes a habit. Over time, your mind automatically redirects sexual sparks into constructive channels.

This can reduce idle daydreaming (or phone scrolling) and add a dash of excitement to your daily grind.

3. Comedic Angle

If you feel a mild flutter of desire while, say, vacuuming, you can grin and think, "Time to supercharge these chores!" Embrace the silliness life's more fun that way.

13.2 At Work: Harnessing Professional Drive

1. Pre-Meeting Spark

If you notice a subtle jolt of arousal maybe from a flirty text or an attractive colleague (be mindful of boundaries!) pause for 30 seconds.

Breathe it in, imagine channeling that energy into clarity and confidence for your upcoming meeting or presentation.

Walk in with that extra pep in your step, letting your "blue ball tension" become a comedic secret weapon for persuasive speaking.

2. Task Sprints

Next time you feel a mild wave of desire at your desk, set a timer for 15 minutes and **plow through** a chunk of work emails, coding, spreadsheet mania, whatever.

Reward yourself with a short break afterward, noting how harnessing that spark gave you a burst of focus.

3. Avoiding Overstep

Keep it internal. Sexual transmutation at work is about channeling your own energy, not making anyone uncomfortable.

If an office crush intensifies your arousal, use it discreetly for motivation, not for crossing professional boundaries or harassing them.

Cheeky Note: Think of mild arousal as your personal "espresso shot" for the office free, potent, and surprisingly fun if handled responsibly.

13.3 Household Chores and Errands

1. The Chore Dance

Doing laundry or washing dishes can be mind-numbing. Infuse a bit of sensual flair put on music that makes you sway, let a small spark of desire drive your movements.

Imagine the water or the rhythmic motions as an extension of your energy. Silly? Yes. Effective? Surprisingly so.

2. Grocery Runs

If you feel a tingle of arousal (maybe you spotted an attractive person in the produce aisle), mentally store that energy.

Let it fuel efficient shopping fewer impulse buys, more focus on your list. You'll zip through the store with a playful grin, harnessing that comedic tension for everyday tasks.

3. Errand Pacing

If errands pile up, harness any flicker of desire (or frustration) to power through them quickly.

After each errand, do a quick breath check, noticing how the tension might have propelled you to be more decisive and energetic.

13.4 Social Events and Gatherings

1. Pre-Social Confidence

If you're nervous about a party or networking event, recall a mild sensual memory before walking in. Let that memory inflate your sense of presence.

You'll radiate a subtle charm, grounded in the knowledge that your body's energy is fueling your social grace.

2. Flirting Responsibly

Light flirting can spark mild arousal, which you can redirect into being more conversational or witty.

Just ensure it's consensual, respectful, and not crossing lines. If you sense you're getting too caught up in flirtation, pivot your mind to transmutation "Let me channel this spark into lively conversation or connecting people."

3. Handling Overstimulation

Large gatherings can overwhelm sensitive folks. If you feel anxious or overstimulated, do a quick microcosmic orbit or box breathing. Let any tension or arousal swirl upward, calming your nerves.

This keeps you from shutting down or leaving prematurely, giving you a comedic "blue ball mental hack" for social stamina.

Comedic Perspective: If you catch yourself saying, "I have so much social anxiety, but I'm also weirdly turned on," consider it comedic gold. Smile, redirect that odd combo into a dynamic conversation starter. "I'm feeling a spark maybe I'll compliment someone's outfit with extra enthusiasm!"

13.5 Integrating Transmutation with Physical Activities

1. Exercise and Workouts

If you feel a spark of desire, use it to power a quick set of squats or push-ups. This merges sexual energy with physical exertion, giving you a natural endorphin high.

Runners or cyclists can imagine each stride or pedal stroke channeling mild arousal into stamina. Let the comedic idea of "running off sexual tension" amuse you.

2. Yoga and Stretching

During a yoga session, if you sense a tingle of desire, direct it through your breath and into the pose. This can deepen your mind-body connection, especially in hip-openers or heart-openers.

Approach it as a personal exploration no need to broadcast it to your yoga class. Keep that comedic secret to yourself, fueling your downward dog with a sly grin.

3. Dance and Movement

At home or in a dance class, letting mild sexual energy flow can elevate your performance. You'll feel more embodied, fluid, and confident.

If you sense tension (like "blue ball frustration"), transform it into dynamic moves or playful choreography.

13.6 Mindset Tips for Everyday Transmutation

1. Reminders & Triggers

Place small sticky notes or phone reminders: "Check your spark" or "Breathe desire upward." These subtle cues keep you mindful throughout the day.

After a week, you might notice it's second nature to harness your energy whenever it arises.

2. Comedic Acceptance

Sometimes you'll forget or get too busy. Or maybe you'll try channeling desire while cooking and burn the pasta. Laugh it off. Embrace the comedic chaos of real life.

The point isn't perfection; it's building a playful, flexible approach to sexual energy.

3. Micro-Pivots

If you catch yourself drifting into a random fantasy at an inconvenient time, pivot: "Wait, let me use this moment for a quick 2-minute sprint on my to-do list."

Each micro-pivot is a small victory, reinforcing the habit of turning random arousal into practical outcomes.

13.7 Real-Life Mini-Case Studies: Everyday Transmutation in Action

1. Brianna's Commute

Scenario: Brianna takes a 30-minute train ride daily. She started noticing random daydreams about a cute fellow passenger.

Pivot: Instead of fantasizing endlessly, she used a mild flush of arousal to focus on reading professional articles or brainstorming her side hustle.

Outcome: She turned idle commute time into productive "mindgasmic" sessions, finishing a full business plan in under a month.

2. Devin's Grocery Efficiency

Scenario: Devin dreaded grocery shopping. One day, a random flirty text from a crush hit him mid-aisle. He felt that jolt.

Pivot: He smiled, inhaled, and decided to power-walk the store with laser focus, grabbing everything on his list in record time.

Outcome: He left feeling accomplished, comedic tension intact, and used that leftover spark to cook a healthy dinner with extra flair.

3. Nadia's Social Spark

Scenario: Nadia felt anxious about networking events. She discovered that if she conjured a mild memory of a past fling or sensual fantasy, she arrived feeling warm and confident.

Pivot: She channeled that vibe into making genuine connections, complimenting others' work, and being more open.

Outcome: Her professional contacts expanded, and she left events feeling less drained, more energized.

13.8 Practical Exercises: Day-to-Day Transmutation

Exercise 1: Morning Spark-Setting

1.   **Step 1**: Upon waking, spend 2 minutes doing a short breath or microcosmic orbit.
2.   **Step 2**: If you sense mild arousal, let it build to a comfortable level.
3.   **Step 3**: Affirm: "Today, I'll channel this spark into tackling my top tasks."
4.   **Step 4**: Note any immediate tasks you want to power through first.

Exercise 2: The Errand Burst

1.   **Step 1**: Before heading out for errands, recall a moment of mild desire or read a flirty message from your partner (with consent!).
2.   **Step 2**: Let that warm tingle guide you as you create your errand list.

3. **Step 3**: Move quickly but mindfully, finishing each errand with minimal procrastination.
4. **Step 4**: Post-errand, do a quick self-check: "Did harnessing that spark help me stay focused and upbeat?"

Exercise 3: Bedtime Reflection

1. **Step 1**: Right before sleep, recall any random arousal moments during the day. Did you transmute them or let them pass?
2. **Step 2**: No judgment just observe. "I used that midday spark to finish my report. Nice!" or "I got lost in daydreaming, oops."
3. **Step 3**: Affirm a gentle intention for tomorrow: "I'll stay playful and mindful."

13.9 Conclusion: The Mundane is Your Playground

When sexual transmutation becomes part of your **daily fabric**, life feels more **vibrant**. Suddenly, folding laundry or commuting can be tinged with a playful undercurrent, fueling creativity, focus, and emotional well-being.

Consistency: Small, frequent pivots build a powerful habit.

Lighthearted: Embrace comedic missteps spilling coffee while you tried to harness a spark is a story to laugh about.

Empowerment: Realize that your body's energy is always there, waiting to be guided, even in the most ordinary tasks.

Next up: **Chapter 14**, where we delve into **advanced practices, rituals, and spiritual traditions** for those craving deeper or more esoteric explorations. Ready to push the boundaries of your *mindgasmic* journey? Let's go!

CHAPTER 14

Advanced Practices, Rituals, and Spiritual Traditions: Taking Transmutation to the Next Level

For some, sexual transmutation is a tool for creativity or emotional well-being. For others, it's a **path of mastery** a doorway to deeper spiritual realms, profound personal breakthroughs, or even mystical experiences. If you feel the call to **go further**, this chapter explores **advanced** techniques and rituals drawn from various traditions. Approach with curiosity, respect, and a willingness to laugh at the occasional comedic twists that arise when exploring such potent energy.

14.1 What "Advanced" Means in Sexual Transmutation

1. Depth Over Difficulty

Advanced doesn't necessarily mean "complicated acrobatics" or "Tantric marathons." It's about **depth** sustaining and refining sexual energy over longer periods, or channeling it into more complex spiritual and creative endeavors.

2. Spiritual or Personal Growth Focus

Advanced practitioners often integrate daily meditation, journaling, or spiritual discipline. The goal is less about immediate productivity and more about **long-term transformation**.

3. Potential Risks and Rewards

Deep energy work can stir intense emotions or unresolved traumas. Some experience "energy overload" or "kundalini crisis."

Rewards include heightened intuition, deep self-awareness, and a sense of "universal unity." Tread carefully, balancing ambition with self-care.

Comedic Perspective: Imagine advanced sexual transmutation like riding a dragon. It's exhilarating, but if you're not prepared, you might get singed. Approach with playful caution and a sense of humor.

14.2 Extended Retention and Semen Preservation (For Those with Male Anatomy)

1. Beyond Edging

While edging is a quick approach, extended retention might span days or weeks, intentionally avoiding orgasm to build a **reservoir** of sexual energy.

Practitioners claim it heightens creativity, confidence, and spiritual clarity.

2. Physical and Emotional Effects

Some men report increased focus, stamina, and a certain "glow" or aura.

However, it can also lead to frustration, mood swings, or comedic "blue ball meltdown" if overdone. Self-awareness is crucial.

3. Practical Tips

Gradual Approach: Don't jump from daily orgasm to a month-long vow. Experiment with a few days at a time.

Regular Release: If tension becomes overwhelming or physically uncomfortable, partial or full release might be needed.

Support: Online communities exist (like "NoFap" or semen retention forums), but take advice with a grain of salt everyone's body differs.

Cheeky Note: If you feel like you're about to combust from unspent tension, let comedic relief help you pivot. "Maybe I'll channel this meltdown into painting a masterpiece or scrubbing the entire house top to bottom my 'blue ball blitz' cleaning spree!"

14.3 Advanced Breathwork and Bandha Practices

1. Bandhas (Yogic Locks)

In yoga, bandhas are "locks" that manipulate energy flow. The **mula bandha** (root lock) involves contracting the pelvic floor akin to Kegel exercises.

Combined with sexual arousal, mula bandha can help lift energy up the spine, intensifying mental focus or spiritual insight.

2. Uddiyana Bandha

This "abdominal lock" can create a vacuum in the torso, drawing energy upward. Some advanced Tantric practitioners incorporate it to guide sexual tension from the lower chakras to the heart or crown.

Approach gently practicing bandhas incorrectly can strain muscles or cause discomfort.

3. Advanced Breath Routines

Kapalabhati (Skull-Shining Breath) or **Bhastrika** (Bellows Breath) can be used in synergy with bandhas to rapidly circulate energy.

Start slow, maybe 10–20 cycles, noticing how sexual energy might spike or transform into a vibrant, almost electric sensation in your upper body.

Caution: These are potent techniques. If you feel dizzy, nauseous, or anxious, stop and return to gentle breathing. Some prefer guidance from an experienced teacher before diving into advanced bandhas.

14.4 Rituals from Various Traditions

1. Taoist Jade Egg or Qigong (For Those with Female Anatomy)

The **jade egg** is inserted vaginally to strengthen pelvic muscles, cultivate internal energy, and enhance sexual transmutation.

Qigong sets (like the "Six Healing Sounds" or specialized sexual energy routines) complement this practice, focusing on channeling Jing (sexual essence) into Shen (spirit).

2. Tantric Puja Ceremonies

Couples or groups gather to perform rituals involving chanting, incense, and symbolic gestures of union.

The idea is to transform physical attraction into a **sacred** experience, sometimes culminating in eye gazing, breath sync, or minimal physical contact.

Not all pujas are sexual; some emphasize heart connection over explicit intimacy.

3. Western Alchemical Rituals

Inspired by hermetic or Rosicrucian traditions, some practitioners create symbolic altars with images representing masculine/feminine principles.

During mild or moderate arousal, they focus on "transmuting base desire" into "gold" of higher consciousness, often journaling insights or reciting alchemical affirmations.

Comedic Perspective: If you find yourself in a circle chanting while holding a jade egg, remember to keep a sense of humor. The line between profound and absurd can be razor-thin, and laughter can ground you in authenticity.

14.5 Kundalini Awakening and Chakra Mastery

1. Kundalini Basics (Recap)

Seen as a coiled serpent at the base of the spine, awakening can lead to intense physical, emotional, and spiritual shifts.

Sexual energy often catalyzes kundalini, bridging root (muladhara) and sacral (svadhisthana) chakras to higher centers.

2. Signs of Awakening

Heat or tingling along the spine, vivid dreams, heightened empathy, or emotional releases. Some experience temporary confusion or anxiety.

If these signs become overwhelming, grounding practices (like walking in nature, hearty meals, or comedic self-talk) can help stabilize.

3. Navigating Kundalini Safely

Some seekers prefer guidance from an experienced teacher. Others self-guide with caution.

Overexertion (like combining intense breathwork, bandhas, and extended retention all at once) can lead to "kundalini overload." Listen to your body's comedic signals if it screams, "Enough, buddy, slow down!"

14.6 Long-Term Celibacy and Monastic Traditions

1. Monastic Insights

Certain monks or nuns across faiths (Buddhist, Christian, etc.) practice lifelong celibacy. They often channel sexual desire into prayer, community service, or meditation.

This can yield immense spiritual focus, but it's a **lifestyle** choice, not a quick hack.

2. Modern Adaptations

Some modern folks adopt periods of celibacy 30 days, 90 days, or more to intensify personal growth. They might follow a monastic schedule of meditation, study, and service.

If you try it, define your purpose clearly. Without a clear aim, frustration or comedic meltdown can ensue.

3. Respecting Individual Paths

Celibacy is not superior or inferior to integrated sexuality. It's one path among many.

The comedic angle might be: "I'm on day 25 of no release my house is spotless, I've read five books, and I'm crocheting scarves for everyone I know. This tension is a productivity goldmine!"

14.7 Real-Life Anecdotes: Advanced Practitioners

1. Max's Semen Retention Marathon

Scenario: Max decided to go 60 days without orgasm. He used daily microcosmic orbit, edging without release, and journaling.

Outcome: He reported surges in motivation, a comedic level of restlessness at times, but also a massive sense of achievement. "I felt like a walking power plant," he said.

Caution: He advises newcomers to do shorter stints first to avoid meltdown.

2. Anita's Tantric Puja Journey

Scenario: Anita attended a weekend Tantra workshop with couples. They performed a puja ritual, chanting and exchanging respectful gazes.

Outcome: She described a "profound heart opening," feeling love for everyone present without it being purely sexual. She calls it "the best group hug vibe ever."

3. Dev's Kundalini Activation

Scenario: Dev practiced advanced breathwork daily (bhastrika + bandhas) while also retaining orgasm for weeks. One evening, he felt intense heat surge up his spine, culminating in a momentary out-of-body sensation.

Outcome: Post-experience, he felt more empathetic and connected to nature. He also had to dial back the breathwork intensity to avoid feeling spaced out at work.

14.8 Practical Exercises: Advanced Practice Sampler

Exercise 1: Weekly Retention Cycle

1. **Step 1**: Choose a 7-day window. Commit to no orgasmic release (solo or partnered).
2. **Step 2**: Each day, do a 10-minute microcosmic orbit or flame visualization.
3. **Step 3**: If tension spikes, practice edging or comedic acceptance. If meltdown looms, consider partial release.

4.   **Step 4**: Journal the experience energy levels, mood swings, comedic highlights. Evaluate at week's end.

Exercise 2: Bandha + Breath Fusion

1.   **Step 1**: Warm up with gentle breathing for 2 minutes.
2.   **Step 2**: On each inhale, apply mula bandha (pelvic floor contraction). Exhale, release.
3.   **Step 3**: After 5–10 rounds, incorporate uddiyana bandha by pulling your abdomen inward/upward after exhaling.
4.   **Step 4**: If arousal stirs, direct it up the spine, pausing at the heart or crown. Conclude if dizziness or comedic "I'm about to pop" feelings arise.

Exercise 3: DIY Mini Tantric Ritual

1.   **Step 1**: Create a small altar candles, meaningful symbols, or pictures representing masculine/feminine energies.
2.   **Step 2**: Play soft music. Sit facing the altar. If comfortable, stir mild arousal through breath or memory.
3.   **Step 3**: Recite a personal affirmation: "I unify my desire with my higher purpose."
4.   **Step 4**: End with a short meditation, letting the ritual ambiance settle in. Journal any insights.

14.9 Balancing Advanced Practice with Everyday Life

1. Grounding and Integration

After an intense session (like advanced breathwork or a Tantric ritual), return to normalcy. Eat a meal, chat with friends, or do something mundane.

This grounds you, preventing spiritual or energetic "floatiness."

2. Respecting Personal Rhythms

Some weeks, you might crave deeper exploration. Other weeks, life stress might call for simpler, comedic micro-practices.

Flexibility ensures you don't burn out or resent your spiritual path.

3. Comedic Relief

Even advanced practitioners experience comedic moments like an unexpected bodily sound during a ritual or tripping over a yoga mat mid-bandha. Laughter fosters humility and keeps you from becoming too solemn.

14.10 Conclusion: Embrace the Mystery, Honor the Journey

Advanced sexual transmutation isn't about elitism or proving your spiritual might. It's a **personal** deep dive into the synergy between desire and higher consciousness. Whether you choose extended retention, bandha-based breathwork, Tantric rituals, or a comedic blend of them all, remember:

Self-Awareness: Listen to your body. Overextension leads to meltdown or comedic fiasco.

Intentionality: Know why you're pursuing advanced methods be it spiritual growth, heightened creativity, or personal challenge.

Humor and Compassion: If you find yourself chanting in the dark while clutching a jade egg, a little laughter can keep you grounded in authenticity.

With advanced practices now in your repertoire, our next chapters will tackle **challenges, taboos, pitfalls**, and the **ethical considerations** of sexual transmutation. Because even a comedic, *mindgasmic* approach deserves careful reflection and responsible boundaries. Onward!

CHAPTER 15

Overcoming Challenges, Taboos, and Pitfalls: Navigating the Bumps on Your MINDGASM Journey

We've explored the joys, techniques, and advanced possibilities of sexual transmutation. But no journey is without **speed bumps** moments when shame creeps in, frustration boils over, or cultural taboos block your path. This chapter tackles the **real-world hurdles** you might face, from internal guilt to external judgment, offering tips to keep your *mindgasmic* momentum alive.

15.1 The Landscape of Challenges

1. Internal vs. External Obstacles

Internal: Shame, guilt, self-doubt, over-stimulation, or comedic "blue ball meltdown."

External: Cultural taboos, religious constraints, disapproval from friends or family, workplace misunderstandings.

Recognizing which type you're dealing with helps tailor your approach.

2. A Comedic Perspective

Humor can diffuse tension. If you catch yourself stuck in a taboo spiral like "What if my neighbor finds out I'm harnessing sexual energy for housecleaning?!" laugh at the absurdity.

This comedic lens keeps challenges from becoming insurmountable.

3. Growth Mindset

Each obstacle is a chance to refine your practice. The more you adapt, the stronger your transmutation muscles become. Embrace missteps as learning curves.

15.2 Dealing with Shame, Guilt, and "Is This Wrong?"

1. Origins of Shame

Shame often roots in childhood teachings, cultural norms, or past traumas. Sexuality is frequently framed as taboo, leading to a sense that desire is "dirty."

Recognizing the **source** of your shame is step one.

2. Reframing Desire

Practice daily affirmations: "My sexual energy is a natural gift. I use it wisely."

Pair this with comedic self-talk if you feel guilt creeping in "No, body, you're not naughty for feeling turned on while making coffee. We're just alive and fabulous."

3. Seeking Support

If shame is overwhelming, consider therapy or counseling. A professional can help you unravel deep-seated guilt.

Supportive communities (online forums or local groups) can normalize your experiences, reminding you that you're not alone.

15.3 Overcoming Frustration and Burnout

1. Too Much Tension, Not Enough Release

Extended retention can morph from "empowering" to "agonizing" if overdone. Listen to your body. If comedic meltdown looms, partial release might be the healthy choice.

Alternatively, direct that tension into intense exercise or a creative sprint. Some comedic "blue ball meltdown painting" might become your next masterpiece.

2. Energy Overload

Advanced breathwork or intense daily edging can lead to overstimulation racing thoughts, insomnia, or irritability.

Scale back. Focus on gentle meditations or limit transmutation sessions to a few times a week. Rest is crucial.

3. Burnout in Relationships

If your partner feels pressured to practice transmutation constantly, it can strain intimacy.

Reintroduce playful spontaneity. Not every sexual encounter must be a *mindgasmic* marathon. Some nights, a cozy cuddle or a quickie with zero transmutation goals is just fine.

15.4 Navigating Cultural and Religious Taboos

1. Respect vs. Personal Freedom

Some cultures or religious communities strictly regulate sexual expression. If you belong to one, you might fear judgment or ostracization for exploring transmutation.

Seek a **balance** between honoring your beliefs (or those of your community) and embracing personal autonomy. This can be delicate.

2. Private Practice

Remember, sexual transmutation is an **internal** process. You're not broadcasting your fantasies or forcing anyone to adopt your methods.

If open discussion feels risky, keep your practice discreet. Let comedic mental winks be your secret superpower.

3. Finding Common Ground

Some faiths have mystical traditions (e.g., Sufi poetry, Christian mysticism, Kabbalah) that celebrate divine love or spiritual ecstasy. You might find parallels or adapt transmutation in a way that aligns with your faith.

Comedic Angle: If you're worried about Aunt Martha discovering your "microcosmic orbit routine," imagine explaining it in comedic code: "I do a quick breathing exercise to stay productive." Keep it simple if that's safer.

15.5 Emotional Triggers and Trauma

1. When Transmutation Stirs Old Wounds

Sexual energy can unearth memories of past abuse or trauma. This is common intense arousal can open emotional floodgates.

If you feel triggered, pause. Seek a trauma-informed therapist or counselor. Don't force transmutation at the expense of your emotional safety.

2. Creating Safe Containers

If practicing advanced techniques, set boundaries. E.g., limit sessions to 15 minutes, or do them only when you feel stable.

Use grounding tools (like comedic journaling or a favorite plushie) if anxiety flares.

3. Partner Sensitivity

If you're partnered, communicate triggers or boundaries. A partner who knows your trauma background can support you gently, avoiding accidental re-traumatization.

15.6 Relationship Conflicts and Mismatched Libidos

1. Different Desires, Different Approaches

One partner might be gung-ho about transmutation, the other uninterested or less sexual in general. This can create tension or comedic "I'm too turned on, you're too turned off" standoffs.

Find a middle path maybe occasional partnered sessions or simpler shared breathwork.

2. Avoid Forcing

Sexual transmutation thrives on **consent**. Pressuring a partner to edge or do advanced breathwork can breed resentment.

Instead, invite them kindly: "Wanna try a 5-minute breath sync? No pressure if you're not feeling it." Respect their "no."

3. Open Communication

If mismatched libidos cause strife, a couples therapist might help. Or comedic honesty: "I'm a walking spark plug right now, but I respect your boundaries. Let me channel this tension into painting the hallway."

15.7 The Pitfall of Performance Obsession

1. When Transmutation Becomes a Competition

You might start comparing your "retention streak" or your "Tantric stamina" with others, or measuring how many *mindgasmic* experiences you had this week.

This leads to ego-driven stress, ironically blocking genuine pleasure and growth.

2. Release the Scoreboard

Focus on **quality** the emotional or creative breakthroughs rather than quantity of days without orgasm or hours in edging.

Humor helps. If you find yourself bragging internally "I'm on day 30 of no release!" smile and remind yourself, "This is about personal exploration, not a gold medal."

3. Celebrating Small Wins

Sometimes a single comedic micro-pivot in the grocery store can be as meaningful as a grand retention streak. Both reflect your evolving relationship with desire.

15.8 Handling External Judgment or Criticism

1. Friends or Family

They might label you "weird" if they discover you're channeling sexual energy to vacuum the living room.

Decide how open you want to be. Some prefer a comedic half-truth ("I do a fun breathing technique for extra motivation"). Others are fully transparent. It's your call.

2. Online Trolls or Skeptics

If you share your journey online, expect pushback some find the concept bizarre or immoral.

Engage politely or ignore. You don't owe anyone an explanation for a personal, consensual practice that doesn't harm others.

3. Respectful Boundaries

If critics push too far, kindly but firmly say, "I appreciate your concern, but this practice is personal and beneficial to me."

Maintaining calm composure can be comedic empowerment. You're basically saying, "Yes, I harness sexual energy for good. No, I'm not sorry."

15.9 Real-Life Anecdotes: Overcoming Challenges

1. Tina's Cultural Taboo

Scenario: Tina grew up in a conservative household where any sexual talk was taboo. She discovered microcosmic orbit and stealthily practiced it.

Challenge: Fear of parents discovering her "weird sexual meditations."

Solution: She framed it as "a Qigong exercise for stress relief." Over time, comedic acceptance helped her realize she could honor her family's beliefs while still exploring her path discreetly.

2. Jared's Guilt Spiral

Scenario: Jared was excited about edging but felt intense guilt after each session, recalling strict religious teachings that condemned sexual pleasure.

Solution: He worked with a therapist to separate personal desire from inherited shame. Gradually, comedic self-talk replaced guilt "I'm just using nature's gift to write better poetry, not summoning demons."

3. Ali & Cam's Libido Clash

Scenario: Ali was into daily transmutation; Cam was a "once a week is fine" type. Tension rose.

Solution: They scheduled one partnered session weekly like a date night for mindful intimacy, while Ali did solo transmutation the rest of the time. The comedic tension around "blue balls" turned into playful banter.

15.10 Conclusion: Embrace the Journey, Embrace the Laughter

Challenges, taboos, and pitfalls are **inevitable** when exploring something as potent and often misunderstood as sexual transmutation. Yet each hurdle be it shame, external judgment, or comedic meltdown can become a stepping stone to deeper self-knowledge and growth.

Self-Compassion: If you stumble, offer yourself grace. Humor helps keep you from spiraling.

Respect for Others: Tread carefully with cultural norms, religious beliefs, and partner boundaries.

Stay Lighthearted: A comedic lens can dissolve tension, making obstacles more manageable and less daunting.

Next, in our **final chapter**, we'll address **ethics, boundaries, and professional contexts**, ensuring your *mindgasmic* journey remains respectful, consensual, and fulfilling for everyone involved.

CHAPTER 16

Ethics, Boundaries, and Professional Contexts: Keeping MINDGASM Responsible and Respectful

We've reached the final chapter of our *MINDGASM* saga. You've learned how to harness sexual energy for creativity, relationships, emotional well-being, and even spiritual depth. But with great power comes great responsibility. This chapter focuses on **ethics, boundaries,** and **professional considerations** ensuring your practice remains a **positive** force that respects personal autonomy, workplace rules, and cultural sensitivities.

16.1 Why Ethics and Boundaries Matter

1. **Protecting Yourself and Others**

Sexual transmutation is personal but can intersect with interpersonal dynamics like flirting, workplace crushes, or intimate partnerships.

Clear boundaries prevent misunderstandings or harm, ensuring that you remain ethically grounded.

2. **Maintaining Integrity**

By honoring consent and ethical guidelines, you keep the comedic, lighthearted spirit of *mindgasmic* exploration intact.

Nothing kills the vibe faster than guilt or conflict arising from crossing someone's comfort zone.

3. **Social and Legal Consequences**

In professional or public settings, misapplied sexual energy can lead to accusations of harassment, lawsuits, or damaged reputations.

Being mindful of these stakes ensures your practice remains a **private** and **positive** endeavor.

16.2 Consent, Communication, and Respect in Relationships

1. Partnered Consent

Always ensure your partner is on board with any technique be it edging, advanced breathwork, or comedic "blue ball" tension-building.

If they decline, respect that "no." Sexual transmutation thrives on mutual willingness, not coercion.

2. Ongoing Check-Ins

Even if you've done certain practices before, check in each time. "Are you comfortable if we do a quick breath sync tonight?"

People's comfort levels can shift daily based on mood, stress, or comedic mishaps.

3. Handling Discomfort

If your partner expresses unease mid-session, stop or pivot to a gentler approach.

Apologize if you inadvertently pushed a boundary. Sincere empathy fosters trust.

16.3 Workplace Conduct: Channeling Energy Without Crossing Lines

1. Private vs. Public

Sexual transmutation at work should remain a **personal, internal** process. You're not sharing fantasies or making suggestive comments.

If an office crush sparks mild arousal, discreetly harness it for focus, not for flirting or unsolicited advances. No play in the workplace. Make it a no go zone.

2. Professional Boundaries

Don't discuss explicit transmutation details with colleagues unless you share a close, trusting bond and they consent to such conversations. Even then, caution is wise.

Refrain from turning any workplace tension into sexual tension. The comedic "blue ball meltdown" must stay in your head, not become a reason to corner a coworker in the break room.

3. Harassment Prevention

Sexual energy is **never** an excuse to cross lines. Harassment can ruin careers and harm lives.

If you feel drawn to a colleague, keep it respectful, minimal, and ensure mutual interest. If unsure, focus that spark solely on your tasks. No comedic meltdown is worth a lawsuit.

16.4 Confidentiality and Privacy

1. Solo Discretion

If you live with roommates or family who disapprove, consider practicing meditations or breathwork behind closed doors.

A comedic "I'm just doing yoga, folks!" might suffice if they hear odd breathing patterns.

2. Partner Privacy

If you and your partner do advanced practices, avoid oversharing explicit details with outsiders unless both of you agree.

Even comedic stories about "our edging session last night" can breach your partner's privacy if told without their consent.

3. Digital Footprint

If you blog or post about your journey, be mindful of personal details. Use pseudonyms or keep certain specifics vague.

The internet is forever protecting your future self from comedic regret if your boss or family stumbles upon your "Tantric Jade Egg Chronicle."

16.5 Cultural Sensitivities and Respect

1. Traveling or Living Abroad

Some cultures have strict views on public affection or sexual discussion. If you're practicing transmutation in a region with conservative norms, keep it **private** and respectful.

Avoid comedic oversharing in areas where sexual content might be taboo or even illegal.

2. Religious Environments

If you're in a faith-based community, gauge whether open discussion of sexual transmutation might offend or conflict with established doctrines.

Maintain a comedic "cover story" if needed like "I do breath-based stress management" to avoid drama.

3. Inclusive Language

Recognize that sexual orientation, gender identity, and cultural backgrounds shape people's comfort with sexual topics.

If you share your practice with diverse friends, be mindful of inclusive language. Avoid assumptions about their sexual norms.

16.6 Avoiding Exploitation and Power Imbalances

1. Teacher-Student Dynamics

If you're teaching sexual transmutation to others, maintain professional boundaries. Romantic or sexual advances toward students can be exploitative.

Some comedic disclaimers about "I'm not hitting on you, I'm just showing you how to do microcosmic orbit" might ease tension, but keep a respectful line.

2. Therapeutic Settings

Therapists, coaches, or mentors should never exploit clients' sexual energy. Any intimate or transmutation-related practice in therapy must adhere to strict ethical guidelines.

If a therapist suggests sexual transmutation in sessions, confirm they're trained and ethical. Report any misconduct.

3. Power Roles

Managers or leaders who sense sexual energy with subordinates risk huge ethical breaches if they blur lines.

Channel that tension into leadership tasks, not flirting or pressuring employees. The comedic meltdown of a scandal is no joke.

16.7 Handling Accusations or Misunderstandings

1. Stay Calm

If someone accuses you of inappropriate behavior, remain respectful. Clarify that your practice is private and internal, or that any flirting was mutual and respectful.

Avoid aggression or defensiveness. Comedic meltdown here can worsen the situation.

2. Apologize if Necessary

If you did cross a boundary inadvertently, own it. A genuine apology can defuse tension.

"I'm sorry if my playful vibe felt uncomfortable. I'll be more mindful moving forward."

3. Seek Mediation

In workplace disputes, HR or a neutral mediator can help clarify misunderstandings.

Don't let comedic bravado overshadow serious reflection on how your actions were perceived.

16.8 Real-Life Anecdotes: Navigating Ethical Quagmires

1. Priya's Workplace Crush

Scenario: Priya felt a strong spark for her new coworker. She used that mild arousal to excel in her projects. But one day, she playfully mentioned "sexual transmutation" in front of him. He looked alarmed.

Solution: She clarified, "It's just a breathing technique I do privately for focus sorry if that sounded weird!" They laughed it off. She kept future references comedic but discreet.

2. Tom the Over-Sharer

Scenario: Tom discovered edging and couldn't stop talking about it to his friend group, including details about how he uses "blue ball tension" to clean his apartment. Some friends felt uneasy.

Solution: After comedic pushback, he realized TMI can breach boundaries. He toned down explicit details, focusing on general positivity. His friendships remained intact.

3. Janelle's Spiritual Class

Scenario: Janelle joined a local Tantra group. She noticed the teacher occasionally blurred lines, flirting with students.

Solution: Janelle recognized the power imbalance, politely left the group, and found a more reputable instructor. She avoided comedic meltdown by trusting her gut about ethical concerns.

16.9 Practical Exercises: Ethical and Boundary Setting

Exercise 1: Personal Boundary Journal

1. **Step 1**: Write down what you consider "private vs. sharable" regarding your transmutation practice.
2. **Step 2**: Note any comedic slip-ups in the past did you overshare or accidentally cross a line?
3. **Step 3**: Define how you'll handle future disclosures. E.g., "I'll keep advanced edging sessions strictly personal."

Exercise 2: Workplace Policy Check

1. **Step 1**: Review your workplace's code of conduct. Understand guidelines on harassment, appropriate behavior, etc.
2. **Step 2**: Brainstorm comedic ways to redirect your sexual spark without involving colleagues. E.g., "When I feel flirty, I'll do a quick breath in the restroom, then power through emails."
3. **Step 3**: If you suspect a mutual attraction, keep it respectful and follow workplace dating policies if you ever decide to explore it.

Exercise 3: Partner Communication Template

1. **Step 1**: Sit with your partner (or potential partner). List 2–3 transmutation exercises you enjoy.
2. **Step 2**: Ask them to list what they're curious about or cautious about.
3. **Step 3**: Agree on a comedic safe word or phrase ("We pivot now!") if either gets uncomfortable.
4. **Step 4**: Schedule a short practice session, ensuring mutual readiness.

16.10 Conclusion: Practicing MINDGASM with Integrity

Sexual transmutation is a **potent** practice. Handled ethically and with clear boundaries, it can transform your life without harming others or inviting comedic fiascos. By respecting privacy, maintaining professionalism, and honoring consent, you ensure your *mindgasmic* journey uplifts everyone involved.

Stay Self-Aware: Continually reflect on how your actions affect yourself and others.

Honor Consent: Whether with a partner or in a workplace setting, respect personal comfort zones.

• **Keep It Fun, Not Harmful**: A comedic lens can make mistakes more bearable, but never let humor excuse real boundary crossings.

With these final ethical guidelines in place, you're well-equipped to embrace the full scope of *MINDGASM*. You've learned to harness desire for creativity, intimacy, emotional health, and spiritual insight while keeping it respectful, consensual, and downright entertaining.

Below is a **comprehensive "Mindgasm Toolkit"** designed to **take your practice to the next level,** providing quick-reference guides, worksheets, affirmations, journaling prompts, and more. It consolidates the best of *MINDGASM* into an **easy-to-use** set of resources, ensuring you can seamlessly apply sexual transmutation in daily life **with humor, consent, and creativity** at the forefront.

THE MINDGASM TOOLKIT

Table of Contents

1. **Quick-Reference Exercise Guide**

2. **Daily/Weekly Checklists and Journaling**

3. **Affirmations and Mantras**

4. **Comedic "Meltdown" Strategies**

5. **Partner Communication Templates**

6. **7-Day and 21-Day Challenges**

7. **Resource Recommendations**

8. **Final Words: Embrace the Cheeky Magic**

Use this toolkit as a **grab-and-go companion** whether you need a quick breath technique at work or want to plan a 7-day retention experiment. Let's dive in!

1. Quick-Reference Exercise Guide

1.1 Core Solo Techniques

1.2 Partnered Exercises

1.3 Quick Fixes (1–2 minutes)

5. **30-Second Arousal Redirect**: When desire strikes unexpectedly, inhale it in, exhale it into a quick mental task (like drafting a short email).
6. **"Spark & Sprint"**: If you feel a flutter, set a 10-minute timer to tackle a chore or write a page of your book.
7. **Box Breathing**: Inhale 4s, hold 4s, exhale 4s, hold 4s imagine mild arousal fueling each phase.

2. Daily/Weekly Checklists and Journaling

2.1 Daily Mindgasm Checklist

Morning

8.   **2-Minute Wake-Up Breath**: Microcosmic orbit or flame visualization.
9.   **Set an Intention**: "Any spark I feel goes into my top goal."

Midday

10.   **Micro-Pivot**: If arousal arises, channel it into a 5–10 minute work sprint.
11.   **Check Energy Level**: Scale of 0–10. Are you a comedic meltdown risk or in the sweet spot?

Evening

12.   **Reflection**: Did you harness any desire? Did comedic mishaps occur? Laugh and learn.
13.   **Solo or Partnered Practice?** (Optional) 5–15 minutes of an exercise that suits your mood.

2.2 Weekly Reflection Prompts

14.   **"Which moments of mild arousal did I catch and transmute effectively?"**
15.   **"Did I face any comedic meltdown or frustration? How did I handle it?"**
16.   **"What new technique did I try, and what was the outcome?"**
17.   **"Am I feeling more creative, focused, or connected?"**
18.   **"What boundaries or ethics did I reinforce this week?"**

3. Affirmations and Mantras

Use these **short statements** to **reframe** your mind when tension or shame surfaces. Feel free to add comedic flair.

1.   **"My sexual energy is a gift, fueling my life's passions."**
2.   **"I respect my desires and channel them wisely, with humor and grace."**
3.   **"Blue ball frustration? I redirect it into brilliant ideas."**

4.   **"I deserve pleasure and productivity both can coexist playfully."**
5.   **"Consent, respect, and comedic acceptance guide my MINDGASM journey."**

Pro Tip: Repeat them during breath holds, or write them on sticky notes. Let comedic self-talk lighten any tension.

4. Comedic "Meltdown" Strategies

Even the best of us hit comedic meltdown: the "I'm so turned on, I can't think straight!" scenario. Here's how to defuse or redirect:

1.   **Name It**: Say (mentally or aloud), "Ah, meltdown approaching. Time to pivot."
2.   **Laugh at the Absurdity**: "Really, body? We're in line at the post office."
3.   **Choose a Strategy**:
1.   **Quick Release**: If you're alone and comfortable.
2.   **Micro-Task**: Channel it into finishing a 10-minute chore.
3.   **Physical Movement**: A quick set of push-ups or a brisk walk.
4.   **Reward the Pivot**: Celebrate with a comedic note in your journal: "Meltdown #2: Conquered by vacuuming the living room!"

5. Partner Communication Templates

5.1 "Let's Try Something New" Script

You: "Hey, I've been exploring this idea of using our sexual spark for creativity/connection. Are you open to a short exercise tonight like 5 minutes of breathing together?"

Partner: [Responses vary if they're hesitant, be understanding.]

You: "No worries if it's not your vibe right now. I just want us to explore new ways to feel close or get creative. We can keep it playful and see how it goes."

5.2 "I'm Feeling Uncomfortable" Script

You: "I want to pause. I'm sensing some tension that doesn't feel good. Can we breathe together for a moment, or shift gears?"

Partner: "Absolutely, let's slow down."

You: "Thank you for respecting my boundary. I appreciate it."

5.3 "Comedic Blue Ball Chat"

You: "So, I've got this comedic tension building feels like I'm ready to explode. But I want to channel it. Could we do a quick 'tease & pause' session and then see if we can direct it into brainstorming date ideas?"

Partner: [Laughter, hopefully] "Sure, as long as we can pivot if it gets too intense!"

6. 7-Day and 21-Day Challenges

6.1 7-Day Mindgasm Challenge

5. **Day 1**: Pick one **solo** exercise (e.g., Microcosmic Orbit). Practice 5 minutes.
6. **Day 2**: Add one **quick fix** pivot at work or errands. Journal results.
7. **Day 3**: Try a **partner** exercise if possible (Synced Breathing).
8. **Day 4**: Incorporate **edging** or mild retention. Notice comedic frustration or success.
9. **Day 5**: Use comedic meltdown strategy once intentionally pivot a meltdown into a creative or chore sprint.
10. **Day 6: Reflect** on shame or guilt triggers. Write a comedic self-compassion note.
11. **Day 7**: Summarize progress. Are you more mindful, playful, or creative?

6.2 21-Day Transmutation Deep Dive

For those wanting a longer experiment:

12. **Weeks 1–2**: Focus on daily **mindful breath** (5–10 minutes) + short **solo** or **partner** exercise.

13. **Week 3**: Attempt extended retention if curious, or advanced breathwork. Keep comedic meltdown strategies handy.
14. **Final Reflection**: Document any shifts in your creativity, emotional resilience, or comedic approach to tension.

7. Resource Recommendations

7.1 Books and Authors

15. **Think and Grow Rich** by Napoleon Hill: The classic text that introduced many Westerners to "sexual transmutation."
16. **The Multi-Orgasmic Man/Woman** by Mantak Chia: Taoist-based guides for harnessing sexual energy.
17. **Tantra: The Supreme Understanding** by Osho: A modern, if controversial, take on Tantric principles (read with discernment).
1. **7.2 Websites and Communities**
2. **Online Forums** (e.g., Reddit communities like r/NoFap or r/SemenRetention): Take advice with a grain of salt look for comedic and balanced discussions.
3. **Mindfulness Apps**: Many offer breathwork or meditation courses that can be adapted for sexual transmutation (Calm, Headspace, Insight Timer).

7.3 Professional Guidance

4. **Therapists or Coaches**: Seek out sex-positive or trauma-informed professionals if deeper issues arise.
5. **Yoga or Qigong Instructors**: Some specialize in sexual energy cultivation check credentials and ethical reviews to avoid comedic meltdown from unscrupulous teachers.

8. Final Words: Embrace the Cheeky Magic

The *MINDGASM* journey is part science, part art, and part comedic escapade. This toolkit:

6. **Simplifies** the array of techniques into quick references and checklists.

7. **Encourages** daily journaling and playful self-awareness.
8. **Offers** comedic meltdown solutions, partner scripts, and advanced challenges.

Remember: **sexual transmutation** is about channeling your innate spark into everything you do, be it writing a novel, strengthening a relationship, or finding joy in grocery shopping. Keep it **consensual**, **respectful**, and **lighthearted**. When in doubt, laugh at the absurdity, pivot that tension into productivity, and celebrate the small wins.

Here's to your ongoing *MINDGASM* journey may it fuel your creativity, deepen your connections, and add a dash of cheeky magic to each day. Happy transmuting!

www.ingramcontent.com/pod-product-compliance
Lightning Source LLC
Chambersburg PA
CBHW071547040426
42452CB00008B/1105